SUCCEED UNDER PRESSURE

To Matthew

Be "GREAT"

Gary Barr

SUCCEED UNDER PRESSURE
CONVERTING FOOTBALL LESSONS INTO BUSINESS SUCCESS

GARY BAILEY
WITH RAKESH SONDHI

Published by Zebra Press
an imprint of Random House Struik (Pty) Ltd
Company Reg. No. 1966/003153/07
Wembley Square, First Floor, Solan Road, Gardens, Cape Town, 8001
PO Box 1144, Cape Town, 8000, South Africa

www.zebrapress.co.za

First published 2012

1 3 5 7 9 10 8 6 4 2

PUBLISHER: Marlene Fryer
MANAGING EDITOR: Ronel Richter-Herbert
EDITOR: Beth Housdon
PROOFREADER: Ronel Richter-Herbert
COVER DESIGN: Sean Robertson
TEXT DESIGN: Monique Oberholzer
TYPESETTER: Monique Oberholzer

Set in 10 pt on 16 pt Stone Serif
Printed and bound by Interpak Books, Pietermaritzburg

ISBN: 978 1 77022 478 0 (print)
ISBN: 978 1 77022 479 7 (ePub)
ISBN: 978 1 77022 480 3 (PDF)

Contents

Acknowledgements

I would like to thank Gary and Dan Nicholl for being such a great inspiration in the writing of this book. Gary and I had been discussing this concept for a number of years, and Gary provided great focus in ensuring that we had a good end-product. Dan's writing and ideas added a unique element that Gary and I would have struggled to deliver.

I would also like to thank Thomas Scarth, our researcher, for key aspects of the book. Thomas dedicated a huge amount of time just after having graduated in Sports Science and Management from Nottingham Trent University. He showed an excellent attitude and was a valuable member of the team.

No acknowledgements page would be the same without a show of gratitude to the people who inspire me on a daily basis: my family – my wife Suman, my children Arjun and Nikisha, and our parents. They are my life!

For 50 years I have followed what is, for me, the greatest team in the world. They make a bad week good, or a good week bad, depending on the results, but my passion for Manchester United will always be with me and shape my thoughts. I am grateful for having been alive during one of the greatest periods of the team's history and to have had an opportunity to study a true legend such as Sir Alex Ferguson.

RAKESH SONDHI

Acknowledgements

Is it really more than three decades since a wide-eyed kid arrived in Manchester hoping to play football? It seems like only yesterday, but all the memories that came flooding back during the writing of this book made me realise that it must have been a long time ago, or I would not have managed to squeeze so much in! The creative process has been a nostalgic one, and it has reminded me of how grateful I am for the career I've had. It's also reminded me of the lessons I've learnt, and for that I thank Sir Alex Ferguson, not just for his kind words in the Foreword or for the time I played under him, but also for the example he has set as a manager and leader.

Professor Rakesh Sondhi would have played for England if passion alone were the prerequisite. He's a superstar in academic circles, however, and his advice and counsel have been invaluable, both in my studies under his guidance and in the writing of this book. His insight is refreshing, accurate and inspiring, and this book would not have happened without him. Thank you, Rocky, for everything.

I first met Dan Nicholl when we worked together with Marcel Desailly and Arsène Wenger during the World Cup in 2010. He is a fine writer and his style of writing is one I greatly admire. He strung together my anecdotes and insights with Rocky's academic understanding to give you the finished product. Thanks to David Williams for casting a final glance over proceedings, and to Zebra Press (an imprint of Random House Struik) for their immense help in getting the book to look so professional

I'd also like to thank SuperSport for making it possible for me to work on TV for the last 20 years and stay close to the game I love; and to also enjoy the company of many other passionate ex-footballers.

A huge thank you to my children, Lara, Jenna, Ross and stepson Luke, who continue to light up my life and mean more than an FA Cup medal or an away win at Anfield ever could; and to Michelle, for coming off the bench early in the second half of the life of Gary Bailey, and having such a magical impact.

And finally to my dad Roy for the love that resulted in many committed hours of coaching, which ultimately provided me with the solid goalkeeping skills that enabled me to play for the greatest club in the world.

GARY BAILEY

Foreword

It gives me great pleasure to write the foreword to a book from one of my former players, Gary Bailey – and not an autobiography, as is usually the case, but a book on leadership and business that engages, stimulates and offers genuine insight from a football perspective. And all this from a goalkeeper!

Goalkeepers are usually the crazy members of a football team, but while Gary had his moments (as I don't need to remind him!), he was a calm, focused, determined servant of United, and a player I was sad not to have had at Old Trafford with me for a little longer. He is remembered fondly by United fans, and his passion for the club shines through in this book, which takes its cue from the challenges and opportunities of football and translates them into principles for the business leader.

The parallels between football and business are extensive, as Gary and his co-author, Professor Rakesh Sondhi, have outlined: we have matches to win and fans to keep happy, while businesses have products to sell and clients to satisfy. And with football itself having become one of the largest, most vibrant industries in the world, the examples and inspiration that the game provides for anyone involved in the broader business environment makes this particular read an invaluable companion.

I'm honoured that Gary and Rakesh have chosen to take my time at Old Trafford as an example of leadership under pressure. I'm also pleased to see the inclusion of my old friend and managerial sparring partner Bobby Robson in these pages. Bobby was a great leader, and the breadth of his success can be appreciated all the more in the context of this book.

The pages that follow offer simple, concise points based on common sense and experience. This falls in line with the management style I've always looked to embrace. I've been in football long enough to understand that the challenges vary but the pressure remains consistent; those in the business world experience a similar environment and will appreciate the nature of the leadership pressures that result.

Few sportspeople experience the consistent pressure of a top-flight professional goalkeeper. Gary Bailey has over 370 games for United behind him, and also an MBA.

Professor Rakesh Sondhi is a most able lieutenant in guiding you through the art of leadership under pressure. I've enjoyed the read, and although I'll not tell Gary, I might even have learnt a thing or two along the way. I have no doubt that you will as well.

SIR ALEX FERGUSON

Introduction

Books by footballers, by and large, fall into two broad categories. The first is the racy, detailed biography, the first instalment of which is usually published when the player in question is barely out of his teens. It details romantic entanglements with lingerie models, the hardship of getting by on £50 000 a week, and the occasional game of football. The second is a more authentic tome: the reflective piece that looks back on an entire football career, tracing the highs and lows that a lengthy devotion to the professional game will inevitably produce.

Those of you who are expecting a racy exposé or a contemplative analysis of my football career may be disappointed. Despite my best efforts as an enthusiastic young member of the Old Trafford staff, I'm decidedly short on lingerie models; and while I'm immensely proud of my football career and achievements, writing a footballing autobiography is not an exercise I feel the need to take on. Instead, you're getting something you might not expect from a footballer: a book on performance under extreme pressure, and how you can use football's example to enhance your own ability to deal with pressure in your life and your business.

Since completing my MBA after playing for Manchester United, I've had an enduring interest in the relationship between business and football, and the business lessons that can be learnt from football. The game was big enough when I played at Old Trafford, but the industry today is an entirely different monster. Cristiano Ronaldo's £200 000-a-week salary, compared to my wage of £300 in the 1980s, is one indication of the staggering changes that have occurred in the football world.

When I was playing for United, I had the chance to work with a man who arrived in Manchester having had some success in the Scottish league. He came with a whispered reputation for having a temper, and faced the prospect of a short tenure at United before joining a pile of discarded managers. Instead, nearly 30 years after arriving at Old Trafford, Sir Alex Ferguson is still at the helm, and has created a footballing legacy that makes him the greatest manager the game has seen.

Lest non-United fans drop the book immediately, this is not a tribute to Sir Alex and his footballing achievements. Rather, it is a look at his enduring success, and at what has enabled him to hold on to one of the most demanding and uncompromising jobs in the world for as long as he has. There are other managers to learn from, too – Sir Bobby Robson, for example, my manager when I represented England at the World Cup; Pep Guardiola, who created an exceptional team at Barcelona; and a number of others who have had a considerable impact, including Arsène Wenger, José Mourinho, David Moyes and Roberto Mancini. But in a job where tenure is frequently measured in months rather than years, the sheer length of Sir Alex's time in charge sets the framework for the discussion that follows.

Top-level football is one of the most stressful and competitive areas of the business world. About 30 per cent of all the managers in English professional football are sacked or resign every year. No other business has that attrition rate. So how do they cope with the pressure, and how can we learn from them? That's what this book is about – and it's for everyone, no matter what your level of leadership in business or whether you're looking to learn how to cope under pressure in your personal life.

> *Top-level football is one of the most stressful and competitive areas of the business world*

What has amazed me, during these difficult times of recession and financial pressure, is that companies spend vast amounts of money and time on reskilling, downsizing, searching for new markets, and so on, but they devote very few resources to helping their management teams and staff deal with the pressure. I know from my time in football that pressure can destroy the most talented and inspire the most average. Many times I've had to drag a player out of the toilets moments before a big game because he was physically sick from nerves. Then I consider the likes of Roy Keane, a legendary captain of Manchester United. Although he didn't have the footballing skills of a Ronaldo, he loved the heat of the battle; it was the opportunity to compete that inspired him, transforming him into an influential player. Much the same applies to John Terry at Chelsea.

As a former Manchester United player, my phone rang off the hook in the hours after the spellbinding finish to the 2011/12 English season. Gleeful fans of Manchester United's rivals were only too happy to remind me that my old team had lost out to Manchester City in the dying moments of the English Premiership's final day. Much as I was disappointed to see United lose, the overall result was one I couldn't quibble with: it had created an extraordinary spectacle that was a vivid reminder of just how strong the Premiership football product is. It was a phone call the following day, however, that remains with me most clearly – a call from my mate Pete, who gave an unexpected breadth of perspective to the English season's coming to an end.

Pete is an Englishman living in South Africa, and he is a massive football supporter. But he doesn't support Liverpool, or Arsenal, or Chelsea, or Spurs, or either of the Manchester sides; no, Pete is the only York City fan I've met in South Africa (and quite possibly the world), and his call to me was to tell me excitedly that his mighty York City warriors had seen off Luton Town in the Conference play-off final, thus guaranteeing them a return to Football League Two – effectively the English fourth division – after an eight-year absence. With the rest of the world still talking in disbelief of the Premiership's crazed finish, Pete was beyond euphoric simply because York City had beaten Luton Town – two teams most of the footballing world has never heard of, and my friend was just as happy, if not more so, than the Manchester City fans I'd encountered after they'd won the league.

Pete's call said a couple of things to me. Firstly, it told me not to answer the phone if he called at any point in the following six months – he'd only be talking about one thing. (In 1995, York beat United 3-0 in a League Cup game. I still get a message on 20 September every year reminding me of the result. There are insurance telesales agents less persistent than Pete.) Secondly, and more importantly, it illustrated just how deep the passion for football runs in England. The passion is religious – and if it's boiling over in the Conference play-off, the bottom end of England's professional spectrum, then the world's getting swept up in the Premiership grand finale shouldn't be that much of a surprise.

Why the reference to Pete and his fanatical York support? Just as football has a place for both York City and Manchester City, so business has its multinationals and its corner stores – and there are shared principles. The resources, the finances and the scale of operations may differ, but at an elemental level the Premiership club and the global brand are chasing success just as much as the League Two struggler and the family business are. What differs is the *definition* of success, not the desire to achieve it. If you look at the targets of the two teams or organisations, the difference will be extreme; if you break down the process required to reach those targets, however, you'll see that they are similar. I hope you'll find relevance in the lessons offered in this book, whether your company is a Manchester City or a York City, whether you're leading a multinational or you're a one-man show.

There is an academic aspect to this extended lesson in leadership under pressure: a football-mad professor who played a crucial role in my own education. It was he who provided the final inspiration I needed to write this book. My good friend Professor Rakesh Sondhi, who oversaw my MBA at Henley Business School and kept me awake through most of my lectures, is sought after internationally for a sharpness of mind that I didn't encounter too often on the football field. As co-author of *Succeed under Pressure*, this is what he has to say:

In writing this book, we spent considerable time thinking about leaders and leadership. These are vast subjects, covering harder areas, such as strategy, and softer areas, such as motivation and communication. We felt, however, that sport adds a unique dimension to the theory of leadership. In all sports the level of competition is intense, and the need to achieve a clearly defined positive outcome is essential. In fact, the failure to deliver this positive outcome can lead to premature dismissal, sometimes at huge cost, as evidenced by the sacking of André Villas-Boas at Chelsea in March 2012. By contrast, a leader such as Sir Alex Ferguson has not only maintained the highest standards for over 25 years, but he has adapted to a dynamic and increasingly pressurised environment.

As an experienced global strategy and leadership consultant, and having worked in strategy development roles for global corporations such as Prudential and Massey Ferguson, I have spent considerable time thinking about the key ingredients for sustainable success.

The role of leadership in the achievement of success is critical. Jim Collins, in his book *Good to Great*, identified leadership as the key common factor in companies that were able to outperform the market for 15 years or more. His research clearly reflects an interest in some of the questions we consider in this book: How do some businesses continue to grow at exceptional rates in highly competitive and uncertain

The role of leadership in the achievement of success is critical

environments? In particular, how do leaders deliver under the increasing pressure that is the result of this competitiveness and uncertainty?

I first 'met' Gary Bailey in 1978 (though he's unlikely to remember me) while standing in the Stretford End – the West Stand of Old Trafford – as an 18-year-old. Gary was making his debut in goal against Ipswich Town, and I enjoyed the thought of my team having a goalkeeper who looked like a goalie, could catch a ball and could keep a clean sheet. (A week before, United had lost 5-1 to Birmingham City; our goalkeeper had been terrible.) Anyhow, as a regular traveller to Old Trafford I appreciated the ability of this blond South African giant. He made a great last-minute save in the 1983 FA Cup final that helped his team to win the Cup. I remember Gary having to retire due to injury at 28, and admire his resilience in returning stronger after failure.

Gary had the privilege of playing at United under three quite different managers: Dave Sexton, Ron Atkinson and Sir Alex Ferguson. The job of managing Manchester United has always been seen as the biggest job in British football. This is largely due to the pioneering style of Sir Matt Busby in taking United into the European Cup in 1956, despite protests from the Football Association, and to the global support gained by the club following the Munich air crash in 1958, when seven players were killed. Manchester United was widely recognised as a pioneer in British football, and even during its downturn in the 1970s and 1980s, it commanded the biggest attendances, week in and week out.

Dave Sexton was a great coach, but a quiet and reserved man who lacked the ability to adapt to the pressures of managing one of the largest sports teams in the world. Ron Atkinson was a big character and one of the lads, which worked well for a while. He came very close to delivering the elusive championship title and he did win the FA Cup twice, but Atkinson did not provide the consistency necessary for sustained success. Sir Alex Ferguson also had his share of challenges early on, but noticeable from the beginning of his tenure was his ability to adapt, and to think of the longer-term needs of his team. The fact that Gary spent time with all of these managers gives him a unique perspective.

As it happened, after having watched Gary from the stands for years, I became his tutor for his MBA dissertation. I was travelling out to South Africa three or four times a year on a variety of projects and got to know him well. It was clear that he possessed an aptitude for speaking and analysis. We spent considerable time talking about a range of topics (not just football!), and developed a close friendship. He also did very well in his MBA. That, coupled with our knowledge of and interest in sport and business, pushed us to explore what we could learn from each other.

I started to design and deliver, to senior management in global companies, leadership programmes that used football as a vehicle of learning. They involved classroom learning in the morning and five-a-side football in the afternoon. Gary and I delivered these programmes, which proved very successful and ultimately led us to conceptualise this book.

I've seen two very different sides to my co-author. There's Professor Sondhi, the composed, eloquent academic whose understanding of leadership and the business world has captivated audiences around the globe. And then there's Rakesh, in his football shirt, pointing out to the referee from 10 rows back that he might have made a mistake and that he'd like to meet him outside the stadium afterwards to discuss the decision in a little more detail. It's a combination, in short, that serves the purpose of this book perfectly: a passionate knowledge of football coupled with an intimate awareness of leadership and the business environment. And in that position, as he explains, Professor Sondhi is ideally placed to appreciate the reasons behind Sir Alex's success, and what we can learn from it:

Sir Alex has been successful in a most challenging environment, where the lives of millions of people around the world are affected by what happens to their football team on match day. For many supporters, a good week is ruined when their team loses, and a bad week becomes good when their team wins. The manager requires strong leadership skills to ensure that he does not succumb to the pressure and get sucked into the emotions and tensions on the day.

Pressure manifests itself in different ways. Some people respond well to the intensity of the situation; others don't. The penalty shoot-out in football is an ideal example of this. A certain amount of pressure is needed to enhance performance, but too much pressure can increase doubt and lead to failure.

Success is defined as a favourable outcome of something attempted. It is also the achievement of a preset goal. Success for Bolton Wanderers or Wigan Athletic in the English Premier League might be avoiding relegation, for example, whereas finishing anything less than top of the league is considered failure for Chelsea or Manchester City. Stakeholders set different targets at the beginning of a campaign, but success brings its own demands: once a target is achieved, expectations are raised (something I suspect many managers of English clubs quietly seethe about when looking back at United's treble in 1999). Therefore success needs to be viewed from both a short-term and a long-term perspective. Smaller goals achieved on a regular basis can have a more positive and encouraging impact than larger goals achieved less frequently.

Smaller goals achieved on a regular basis can have a more positive and encouraging impact than larger goals achieved less frequently

A great example of this lies in the experience of my old United team-mate Steve Coppell, who has had wonderful success managing smaller teams and getting the best out of them. During his time at Reading, which he had somehow wrestled into England's top-flight Premier League, he found himself at the helm of a team fighting a grim battle with relegation – hardly surprising, given the size of the club and the minimal resources available. Coppell's task, then, wasn't just to avoid going down, but to keep spirits up in a depressing environment, bearing in mind that the league table would usually show Reading near or in the relegation zone.

To do that, Coppell scrapped the display of league tables in the dressing room and at the club and drew up his own short-term version instead. He'd sit down with the players and look at their next five games, and together with them decide on a reasonable assessment of chances. Away to Liverpool? A point would be nice, but defeat was realistic. Home to Wigan? A game that should be won if avoiding relegation was to be achieved. Away to Villa? Should manage a draw at least. The points target for the upcoming five matches would then be set, and Coppell's new table would show performance against expectation, as opposed to performance in relation to the whole league, where the teams above them had different expectations. It gave his players a far more positive and realistic set of parameters, and his methods proved successful.

Managers and business leaders have to get the best out of their people. After all the jibes directed at Spanish superstar Fernando Torres after his move from Liverpool to Chelsea, or Andy Carroll after leaving Newcastle for Liverpool, you have to ask questions about their dramatic loss of form. Without necessarily absolving the player in question of blame (and I'd have a hard time doing that with Chelsea or Liverpool fans), you have to ask whether the new environment and the new management are partly responsible for the downturn in performance. When you've just spent in the region of £50 million on a player, you can't afford to write off barren performances purely as a loss of form – you have to get the best from this expensive member of staff.

Success (or lack thereof) in the case of a Torres or a Carroll can so often stem from the mental state of a player. Brian Clough, a colourful, enigmatic football boss, once famously appeared in the

Nottingham Forest dressing room at half-time, with his side trailing. He stuck his head around the door and apologised to the team, saying it was his fault for selecting the wrong team, before turning around and walking off. Stung into action, Clough's reverse psychology worked brilliantly: Forest came back to win that game.

According to Gary Pallister, the great centre half for Manchester United in the 1990s, Sir Alex would put four or five names in an envelope at the beginning of each season (or so the manager said). These names were the ones he believed would not live up to the demands of the season ahead and might have to leave. Although they thought it was a tactic used to wind them up, says Pallister, none of them wanted to take the risk of not performing, so they all tried even harder. This is a great example of mental inspiration by a manager.

Another kind of mental inspiration is superstition. It has a powerful hold in many cultures; it's just the approach that varies. When I first arrived at Manchester United, the players wouldn't let me put my shoes on a table, open an umbrella indoors or walk under a ladder. In South Africa, before I went to England, my university team (I was at Wits University) was allowed to play against Kaizer Chiefs – a match that in 1977 was rare, as apartheid was at its most intense and Kaiser Chiefs were an all-black team.

I had bought the most expensive goalkeeper gloves from England (all my student money and more had gone towards them) and I proudly put them in the back of the net with my cap. I had a rather good game. With 10 minutes to go, we were desperately holding on to a 1-0 lead and I was keeping everything out. Then a Chiefs fan scaled the fences, grabbed my gloves and ran off with them, as he – and the rest of the fans – believed that these gloves were stopping any goals from going in.

I tackled the perpetrator, retrieved the gloves and, without thinking, returned them to their place in the back of the net. In the minds of the Chiefs fans, I'd just given them the middle finger and ensured that my goal would not be breached. With that, a riot started. In those days the police used a sneeze machine that pumped out tear gas for crowd control, and as we scampered to the tunnel I saw fans scrambling to get away and jumping over the edge of the stands. The point of this story, though, is that their belief was so strong that they were convinced they couldn't score past me with the gloves in the goal. As Professor Sondhi confirms, success is so often a mental issue:

The ability to succeed is partly self-determination – successful people choose to succeed because they want to succeed, not because of external factors. Look at Sir Alex's policy of playing around with the team and making changes during matches in the early part of the season to achieve longer-term goals. There's never a sense of his waiting for things to happen when United plays, and that's a hallmark of the best managers – the ability to make just the right change consistently. This raises another important point about the mental state: a player who is sent on has both the knowledge that his manager believes he's the man to make a difference and the desire to show that he deserves a place in the starting XI. No wonder, then, that a player so inspired frequently does make the difference.

Self-belief is also crucial to success, whether it's the substitute who knows he can change a game or the manager certain that

> *The ability to succeed is partly self-determination – successful people choose to succeed because they want to succeed, not because of external factors*

he's made the right replacement. Successful people believe that they can make desirable things happen – if you don't think your team can win, or that your product can take off, who will? This self-belief encourages the challenging of the status quo. Look at Sir Alex selling Andrei Kanchelskis, Mark Hughes and Paul Ince in the 1995/96 season, decisions that were met with derision from the media but which in time proved inspired, as the young players such as David Beckham, Paul Scholes and Ryan Giggs quickly became the core of an extraordinarily successful team.

And then there's self-confidence, an asset of immense value. When Gary first appeared in my classes for his MBA, I had a quiet chuckle – it was an honour to meet a successful member of the Manchester United team, but a footballer doing an MBA? He wouldn't last. But Gary had immense self-confidence (which, it's crucial to note, is very different from arrogance), and that, coupled with ability, was vital to his completing his MBA with flying colours. Successful people also have a sense of optimism, and Gary was the complete optimist about nailing his degree – even if his professor had initial doubts. For all I taught Gary, he left me with a lesson or two as well.

Footballers not being ideal university material? I can't begin to imagine where the professor got that idea. In truth, the self-confidence wasn't always concrete: an MBA is a tough course, and there was the occasional flicker of self-doubt, but by nature I'm a confident person and I believed in my ability to get through it. Success in football helped. There might not have been much talk about advanced business strategy in the dressing room after an away win at Highbury, but success in one area prompts self-belief in others.

Professor Sondhi explains what we set out to do in this book:

There are certain characteristics an individual needs to possess for effective self-management. Team success follows only if the leader believes in his or her ability to succeed at an individual level.

Team success follows only if the leader believes in his or her ability to succeed at an individual level

Success in business can be ascribed to many factors, but research has generally put one criterion above all others: leadership. But even after many years of research, the magic formula for leadership is still not fully understood, as evidenced by the relatively small number of truly great leaders in business today.

In this book the idea of succeeding under pressure is explored with the objective of developing and presenting a holistic and practical framework for achieving success. In examining these concepts, we draw on the footballing experience of Gary Bailey and his relationship with some of football's greatest leaders, including Sir Alex Ferguson, as well as my business experience as a U.K.-based strategy and leadership consultant.

The international football sector provides a unique environment, where leaders and players have no choice but to perform when they find themselves in a stadium filled with tens of thousands of spectators. The games are the leaders' 'moments of truth' (as Jan Carlzon of Scandinavian Airlines puts it) or 'magical moments' (as the Disney Corporation's Michael Eisner calls them), where excuses for a lack of preparation are not acceptable.

Two core elements are needed to develop the required attributes for successful leadership. The first of these is a combination of drive, passion and commitment. Drive encompasses the will to succeed and the determination never to give in, even under the most stressful of conditions. The second core element is team-based delivery. Team-based sports provide a tremendous foundation for learning about the leadership attributes that are needed to win in competitive situations. Competitive sport also provides a background where performance is assessed in front of thousands of spectators, and participants have no place to hide.

Sometimes it is assumed that people are born leaders. This assumption should be challenged, as development and learning are critical to the evolution of leadership. Very rarely will you find a leader who hasn't made mistakes. Fear, and the poor management of fear, is probably the biggest block to leadership development. Great leaders are not born, but are nurtured by learning from their responses to the challenges presented to them. As these challenges become increasingly difficult, individuals either simply stop putting themselves in those situations, thus protecting themselves from failure, or become stronger and better leaders, learning from their mistakes and successes.

Very rarely will you find a leader who hasn't made mistakes

To capture the attributes of leadership, we have developed an easy-to-remember acronym: LEADS. The model is based on developing personal traits that are intuitive and allow the leader to perform under stress. It breaks down as follows:

L – level-five leadership
E – emotional intelligence
A – adaptability
D – destiny
S – support

Each of these elements will be discussed in the chapters that follow. With all the management and leadership courses on offer today, there is no question that all leaders know what they should be doing and how they should be doing it. However, this does not mean that they actually display these essential characteristics. The development of intuitive attributes is therefore crucial. LEADS involves developing a strategic and holistic perspective that allows the leader to combine professional will, emotional intelligence and adaptability to maximise the impact of decisions taken. Commitment is required from an individual to change and transform: without this desire, the attributes will never be ingrained in the character of the leader.

A vital part of the strategic perspective is the ability to adopt the most appropriate perspective, as while strategic skills are quite easy to apply, applying them at the appropriate level of the organisation is more difficult. The strategy to reach your destiny requires excellent communication and the personal qualities of humility and perceptiveness. Effective communication is the backbone to building support and is about the skills needed to inspire people to give 110 per cent to a cause, which requires the leader to be sensitive and able to engage with people in the organisation.

This book will compare and contrast the qualities of top leaders in football to establish what makes them different, and yet successful in their own terms, starting with Sir Alex Ferguson. Sir Alex, who took over at Manchester United in 1986 and is still going strong, has achieved consistent and sustainable performance over a quarter of a century. In addition, he was successful in breaking the domination of Celtic and Rangers in Scotland during his time at Aberdeen. Over the years Sir Alex has demonstrated a unique ability to adapt his style based on a constantly changing environment.

We'll also look at a manager who has pleased and perplexed his fans in equal measure: Arsène Wenger. He has been great at identifying, growing and believing in talent. While success has been achieved, it hasn't been consistent. Some argue that Wenger's weakness lies in his inability to adapt his style to the demands of a rapidly changing environment. Wenger demonstrates a level of self-belief that may be his strength, but it can also prove a barrier if it isn't coupled with an ability to recognise his shortcomings and adapt accordingly.

Over the years Sir Alex has demonstrated a unique ability to adapt his style based on a constantly changing environment

And then there are the two managers who have dominated the spellbinding football duel that Spain has put on in recent years. José Mourinho is renowned for achieving success very quickly, but he also tends to stay at one place for only a short time. One of the new generation of continental managers, he has a highly fuelled ego that provokes controversy, but can work well with the similarly highly fuelled egos of the players. His rival, Pep Guardiola, has also achieved major success in a short time, but he benefited from inheriting a squad of superbly gifted players. From that he produced a team that played the most complete, beautiful football seen on the continent, and was one of Barcelona's finest managers. But he left the club at the first sign of real pressure, when Madrid won La Liga and Chelsea the UEFA Champions League in 2012, which leaves him yet to prove his ability when his back is to the wall and his team is not achieving.

All of these leaders have had to succeed in high-pressure situations, with enormous expectations placed on them. Their strategies have had to embrace the people factor: in sport, and in football in particular, there is huge focus on ensuring that sportspeople are in the right frame of mind to perform. This is sometimes ignored in the business environment, where leaders often neglect some of the softer aspects of management and then wonder why performance levels are not as high as expected. Football managers simply can't afford to get anything but the best out of a player on £100 000 a week. However, although the wages paid by a business leader may be lower, the approach shouldn't change.

In exploring how to develop the ingredients necessary to deliver success in business environments, this book presents principles that are universal and that rely heavily on a personal commitment to change: the characteristics are learnt through a focused programme of change, which demands time and a conscientious effort to recognise those areas that are in need of development. Such awareness is crucial, as this is the start of the learning process.

> *We are able to change the way we behave provided that we see the importance of the change and understand how it fits into our long-term goals*

According to theories of neuroscience, we are able to change the way we behave provided that we see the importance of the change and understand how it fits into our long-term goals. If we don't comprehend in this manner, the change process is unlikely to prove sustainable. This is also the case with organisations: the individual — not just the leader — has to recognise the need for change in order for desired outcomes to be met. Succeeding under pressure means that we need to be able to perform, from both an individual and an organisational viewpoint, when we are outside of our comfort zones. The development of this ability is critical, and will be dealt with in this book.

Quick wins are an essential part of the change and development process, as they create momentum that inspires us to the challenging of boundaries. This ties in with the setting and meeting of realistic, short-term goals, which provides encouragement in attaining long-term targets. It has to be remembered that failure is not necessarily the non-achievement of a goal, but the act of not trying: non-achievement of a target is an opportunity to learn, while excuses for not trying amount to failure. Thus, with non-achievement you can continue to grow and develop, but you don't move forward at all by refusing to try.

The structure of this book includes opportunities for reflection as part of the developmental process. Periods of reflection will help you to identify how much of a priority certain attributes are for you. The reflection process is based on exploring your inner feelings about certain key elements, and it is enhanced considerably by writing down your thoughts in a logbook, not as bullet points, but in the form of an engaging story where your emotions can be expressed as fully as possible. The writing process allows you to gain clarity and aids in committing to memory your views and reflections, making the change more tangible.

The 'Training Day' section at the end of each chapter provides a series of questions to guide you in your reflection. The questions are designed to help you recognise your own behaviour and to think about your ideal conduct so that the gap between the two may be assessed and closed. Reflection and the writing down of your personal responses are the equivalent of the hours spent practising, working out and preparing for a big game. If you work on these fundamentals and are committed to adapting as required, we believe that you'll be well on track to succeed under pressure.

There is no quick way to develop the attributes described in this book. Permanent attainment of these traits requires hard work and commitment. While we'll support this by providing areas of focus for reflection, ultimately it's up to you to perform when the whistle is blown and the game kicks off.

Enjoy the book; enjoy success!

1

Performance under Pressure

'You see the best out of Sir Alex
not when United are winning, but in
our worst nightmares.'
– Carlos Queiroz, former Manchester United assistant coach

Twelve yards is the most terrifying distance on earth. But not for everyone: it's more likely to be 22 yards if you're an opening batsman facing the new ball in a cricket match, or one yard if that's the distance between you and a charging 120-kilogram lock forward in a game of rugby. But for me, 12 yards was the distance that kept me awake at night and still provides some of the most vivid memories I have of my time as a professional footballer. For 12 yards is the distance I stood from the penalty spot and from a ball that, the odds suggested, was much more likely to end up in the back of the net than not. It was up to me to defy those odds. Occasionally I would make the save, and my team would unite around me in celebration; most of the time I wouldn't, and I'd glare at the defender responsible for the penalty as I retrieved the ball from the net. (If I'd given away the spot kick, I'd glare at the referee instead; he'd clearly made the wrong decision.) But whether I saved it or not, whether my opponent struck the ball into the top corner or sent it soaring into the stands, the pressure of the situation remained constant – and I had to perform under that pressure.

When I was a goalkeeper, I felt that no one in the team was under as much pressure as I was. Strikers could miss a goal, but they might have a chance minutes later to atone for it. Midfielders could send a pass astray or let someone beat them, but that usually didn't change a game. Even defenders could lose the player being marked or get beaten to a header without being held responsible to the degree that a goalie is. As a 20-year-old at Manchester United, I lacked the experience to deal with these situations. (Peter Schmeichel, by contrast, made his Manchester United debut at the age of 28; Edwin van der Sar was well into his 30s.) And then there was the issue of pay. When you're each earning £300 a week and your win bonus is another £100, letting in a late goal could cost your teammates an awful lot of money. No one, it seemed clear to me, had to play football under the same sort of pressure as the goalkeeper.

A couple of decades on, and my views have changed. I still believe that goalkeepers don't get nearly enough credit, and that a top keeper should be worth every bit as much as a top striker in the transfer market. But I've realised that my teammates were under just as much pressure to perform and to produce their best in a league of the world's best players, where they were scrutinised by a most demanding football public. And, more importantly, I've realised that for all the penalties I had to face, all the one-on-ones I had with strikers, all the desperate saves I had to make to preserve a lead or stave off defeat, one person in our team was under considerably more pressure than the rest of us: the manager.

There is no industry in the world that comes close to matching the attrition rate of professional football managers. Such is the overwhelming demand for immediate success that many managers have barely arrived at a club before they're clearing their desks and heading out the door.

There is no industry in the world that comes close to matching the attrition rate of professional football managers

Look at Chelsea's coaches under Roman Abramovich, for example. In the era of the Russian's ownership, Stamford Bridge has made Italian politics look settled in comparison. While you probably have a general appreciation of the managerial merry-go-round, here are a few stories and statistics from Stamford Bridge that illustrate just how brutal an environment professional football is.

Claudio Ranieri arrived in London in 2000. While he might have sounded like an Italian Inspector Clouseau as he grappled with English in his first press conferences, he came with a considerable pedigree, having managed Campania, Cagliari, Napoli, Fiorentina, Valencia and Atlético Madrid – some of Europe's biggest club sides. He was in residence when Abramovich arrived at Chelsea, and took the club to second place – Chelsea's best performance in 49 years – behind an astonishing Arsenal side. But it wasn't enough. With no trophies won, he was sacked in May 2004.

Ranieri was followed by the most colourful of Chelsea's recent appointments, José Mourinho. Never beaten at home, and defeated in just 20 of the 182 matches for which he managed Chelsea, Mourinho won the Premiership (twice), the FA Cup, the Carling

Cup (formerly the League Cup) twice and the Community Shield. He also brought star players to London: Didier Drogba, Michael Essien, Ricardo Carvalho and Arjen Robben, among others. But he was never able to take Chelsea to a Champions League title, and the self-proclaimed 'Special One' eventually appeared to clash with Abramovich; in 2007, Mourinho was gone by mutual consent, despite having achieved remarkable successes.

From there it was on to the brooding Israeli, Avram Grant, who took Chelsea to the Champions League final in Moscow, where he was a John Terry penalty away from winning, but was nevertheless sacked after just a year in charge. He was followed by Luis Felipe Scolari, World Cup–winning coach of Brazil, who was never able to settle properly at Stamford Bridge and was also fired after a year. Dutchman Guus Hiddink, a stopgap appointment, came next. He won an FA Cup, but soon left to honour an earlier promise he'd made to coach Russia.

Carlo Ancelotti, a highly regarded Italian, then arrived after spells at Juventus and AC Milan. He won the Premiership, the FA Cup and the League Cup in his two years as coach, and brought Ramires and David Luiz to Chelsea, but he was also shown the door at the end of the 2010/11 season.

After that came the ignominiously brief reign of André Villas-Boas, who, like Mourinho before him, had arrived on the back of success with Portuguese club FC Porto. That's where the parallel ended, however: Villas-Boas didn't even last one season, leaving former player Roberto Di Matteo to take the club through some almighty battles in Europe en route to the elusive Champions League trophy – which was finally lifted by Chelsea's eighth coach in less than a decade.

Back when I played, a couple of seasons was the least a manager could expect to be given to make his mark and mould a winning squad; today, a couple of months has become the acceptable probation period. It is a measure of the demands now made by professional football on its quicksilver cast: players transfer constantly, but it's the movement of managers that takes the breath away. And that's why managing a big professional football team invites such massive pressure. The pressure has intensified as owners have started to feel that they are falling behind if they delay making decisions. These owners also come from environments where they have seen massive personal gains over brief periods of time. Abramovich, for example, became a multibillionaire very rapidly following the collapse of the Soviet Union, an experience that evidently fuelled his impatience in the football context.

That's why the man I played under all too briefly is the man I've come to admire so openly, and who has become a textbook case study for performance under pressure. The length of Sir Alex Ferguson's reign at Manchester United is amazing. Well into his third decade at Old Trafford, Sir Alex has met the demands of success, juggled the talent and ego that have passed through his changing room, dealt with ownership and boardroom challenges, and secured enduring loyalty from players and fans. All of this he has done consistently since he arrived at Old Trafford in 1986, a time when José Mourinho was a school coach hoping for a big break, Martin O'Neill was playing for Fulham and Pep Guardiola was a 15-year-old kid dreaming of playing for the Barcelona side that he'd go on to manage so successfully. These men are now his contemporaries, some of the best football managers in the game today.

Later in this book there is a comparison between Sir Alex and other leading figures in management, both to illustrate their strengths and to reinforce how United's boss has learnt from his peers and adapted his leadership style accordingly. In particular, my memories of playing for England under Sir Bobby Robson add to the broader picture of successful management.

Sir Bobby Robson survived the managerial merry-go-round for nearly 35 years, having started at Fulham in 1968. His reign, which ended in 2004 with Newcastle, was different from Sir Alex's, in that Sir Bobby was successful at a number of clubs, both in the United Kingdom and in continental Europe. He achieved success at a small club, Ipswich, and in Barcelona at one of the largest clubs in the world. Resilient like Sir Alex, he would get knocked down after leaving a club, but he'd dust himself off and get back up again a more complete manager, having learnt from his experience.

The examples inherent in the success of Sir Bobby, Sir Alex and others make for a template that's readily transferable to the business world. Allow Professor Sondhi, who delighted in putting pressure on *me* when I was doing my MBA under his uncompromising gaze, to take over here:

The examples inherent in the success of Sir Bobby, Sir Alex and others make for a template that's readily transferable to the business world

Pressure takes many forms and manifests itself in different ways, such as increased blood pressure, increased heart rate, muscle tension and intestinal upset. These physical responses to pressure are related to the neurological 'fight-or-flight' response, which is humankind's reaction to a perceived threat. The fight-or-flight response releases two hormones in the brain: epinephrine (also known as adrenaline) and norepinephrine (also known as noradrenaline), which cause the heart to beat faster, increase the respiration rate and blood pressure, and activate blood-clotting mechanisms to prepare for physical injury. One person will see a particular situation as pressurising, while another person will welcome that same situation as a challenge. The pressure – and its physical implications – will either create a winning edge or cause the individual to freeze and thus to fail to deliver. Our perception of the situation is so often the key to managing pressure.

The ways in which pressure manifests itself in the workplace vary. It creates a sense of urgency, which is critical to performance; however, some people fail to respond in a performance-enhancing way. They miss deadlines, make errors and sometimes even ignore the pressurising deadline, which is why good management systems are crucial. Another consequence of pressure is internal organisational conflict: often people blame others in the team for their personal failures.

In sport, good leaders can calm team members and alleviate team stress by placing the pressure on themselves rather than on their team. In that way, the team is free to flourish without having to deal with overwhelming pressure. In the workplace, by contrast, people are often rewarded only on an individual basis. Generally teams in the workplace comprise work groups, where everyone is responsible for doing their own bit in a project. Rarely do such groups

In sport, good leaders can calm team members and alleviate team stress by placing the pressure on themselves rather than on their team

operate as a top team of sportsmen would, working for each other without the presence of ego and playing towards a common vision or goal.

Part of the issue is that we tend to crave external gratification – we want people to applaud and acknowledge us, particularly if we see ourselves as entertainers, as footballers do. However, this also makes us vulnerable to criticism, thereby increasing the pressure to perform. This pressure, of course, can often have a negative impact on performance, which means it is up to the leader to turn what many might take as 'pressure' into a 'challenge', thus transforming a threat into motivation.

Gary illustrates how Dave Sexton, Ron Atkinson and Sir Alex have coped with the considerable pressures of managing United.

I recall Dave Sexton's response to pressure most clearly – and it wasn't great! Dave was an incredibly talented coach with a brilliant football brain, and he could have gone on to become a very successful manager. But Dave simply didn't handle pressure well: he used to lock himself in his office and switch off the lights to get away from the world and to avoid having to talk to anyone. Quite simply, the stress of managing a club like United was too much for him, and that, I'm afraid, negated the rest of the skills he brought to the position. By contrast, Ron Atkinson loved the pressure. I felt that he wasn't able to pay attention to the small details, however, such as players in the reserve or youth teams. When his star players were injured all at once in late 1986, it all fell to pieces.

Sir Alex not only enjoys pressure, but thrives under it. He still has time for small details, and these often make the difference. He knows where his players are and when they are misbehaving, and he ensures that all of his players, from the youth team upwards, are behaving in the manner expected of them.

As mentioned in the Introduction, we use all sorts of methods to help us deal with pressure. In football, superstition is a big one. I benefited from the help of a South African witch doctor, who passed on a padlock through my father, Roy. I had conceded seven goals in three cup final appearances: a 3-2 loss to Arsenal in the

1979 FA Cup final, a 2-1 loss to Liverpool in the 1983 League Cup final, and a 2-2 draw with Brighton in the 1983 FA Cup final. My dad was manager of a club in South Africa – Pretoria Callies – and the witch doctor thought he could solve my problem, hence the padlock. It came with the warning that it could be used only three times and that I had to 'unlock' my goal at half-time (or we wouldn't be able to score), and then lock my new goal at the other end after half-time.

I used the padlock in the 1983 FA Cup final replay against Brighton, which we won 4-0. I was more than happy to make use of it again in the 1983 Charity Shield against Liverpool, which we won 2-0, and then for the last time in the 1985 FA Cup final, where we beat Everton 1-0. I conceded no goals in those three matches. Did the padlock really work, or did it just shore up my self-belief and thus alleviate some of the pressure, enhancing my performance? I'd suggest the latter, although the witch doctor would doubtless disagree.

The question is, what similar methods would help in the business arena? I don't expect analysts at a top investment bank to be looking for the contact details of a witch doctor in South Africa, but holding on to lucky charms, a good-luck card from a spouse or friend, or a family picture might help you to deal with the pressure more effectively.

Pressure exists in all walks of life. I remember battling through my MBA with work during the day and academic study at night. People in business are of course always under pressure to deliver better products, increased market share, higher profits – and sometimes simply to survive, for failure could mean the

Pressure exists in all walks of life

closing of a business and the loss of years of work. However, students and business leaders, unlike footballers, are spared the additional pressure of being constantly in the public eye. Even for listed companies, which have to report regularly and maintain shareholder confidence, the assessment period is, at the very least, a quarter, or three months. What's more, a difficult quarter for a company is rarely enough to provoke full-scale change in the company's management.

Compare that with football, where four bad results in a row – a grand total of a fortnight's play – can result in a manager being shown the door. A business executive isn't on show for 90 minutes a week, televised to hundreds of millions of people, with the finger of a billionaire owner hovering over the trigger if results don't go the right way. This is not to demean the demands of the corporate world, where long hours, demanding budgets and shareholder expectation can make life an unpleasant blur of constant pressure. Rather, it serves to illustrate the brutal immediacy of performance demands in professional football. It's a case of, 'Welcome to the club, great to have you on board, best of luck managing the side – and know that we have your replacement already lined up for next month ...' This, essentially, is why I believe we can learn so much from how successful footballers and football managers handle pressure.

We can learn so much from how successful footballers and football managers handle pressure

My experience as a goalkeeper has added relevance here. Think of your own working experience and add up the number of genuinely career-defining moments you've faced on an annual basis – moments that could have cost you your job, or cost your company a major deal. By that, I really do mean moments, for I had them every week: all it took was for a ball to slip through my legs or elude my outstretched hand. Think back to England goalkeeper Robert Green and the goal he let in while playing against the United States in the 2010 World Cup: the ball went straight through his legs. England drew instead of winning, which put them into a tough knockout game against Germany, which they lost. Green's mistake was therefore a key factor in England's crashing out of the tournament and, undeniably, a career-defining moment for the keeper.

This leads to another related point, and one that Professor Sondhi has made a number of times during discussions of the rueful state of the modern game (if he had his way, I suspect Rakesh would still have us playing with leather balls and three-quarter-length shorts), namely the notion of what constitutes success today. There was a time when a strong finish in the league could sustain the ambitions of a club for a season, with a trophy more than enough cause for celebration. A mid-table finish, but victory in the FA Cup, would be considered a great season, and one that allowed the manager to sit back and accept the plaudits. Today, the situation is very different.

For the big clubs in Europe, a strong showing in one competition but modest achievement in the rest (and there are plenty of them) simply isn't good enough. A strong season now means success in Europe, success in the domestic league and success in a local cup competition – with a victory in at least one of them. And if a London club run by a Russian billionaire is the club in question, then success is defined as winning the Champions League and the Premiership – or the manager is out.

In a way, Sir Alex has to shoulder the blame here. Since 1999, the perception of what is possible has changed. Ambitious owners now have a benchmark that they view as a realistic goal rather than as the remarkable footballing anomaly it was when United somehow won the treble of Premiership, FA Cup and Champions

League. Forgotten is the last-minute miracle in Europe, the good fortune of the FA Cup run and the results pulled off by extremely narrow margins in the league. Instead, a simple maxim has been adopted: If United can do it, then so can we.

Of course, that extends to Manchester United itself. Having been the architect of that most extraordinary season, Sir Alex raised his own bar even higher. Professor Sondhi makes a valuable point here on rival managers, and how relentless pressure has influenced their style:

One of José Mourinho's tactics is to create an 'us-versus-them' situation to obtain loyalty from his players. When Sir Alex has done this with his team, he has pitted Manchester United against everyone else, whereas Mourinho tends to make it all about himself and the players. This has resulted in his managerial successors never being able to control the dressing room, because Mourinho had created powerful bonds with his players. There would be stories about managers who came after Mourinho, such as Luiz Felipe Scolari or André Villas-Boas, not having the support of key players like Didier Drogba and John Terry – and then a few weeks later, these managers would be sacked.

This was certainly the story of André Villas-Boas in the 2011/12 season. The team was doing badly, yet after he was sacked the team won the Champions League and the FA Cup with a temporary manager, Roberto Di Matteo.

Arsène Wenger appears to have the support of his players, but sometimes seems to have lost the backing of his supporters. Wenger is a man of principle, however, and tends to recover. In the 2011/12 season, for instance, Wenger was under attack from the media and the fans for poor performances, but he stuck to his principles of playing a certain kind of football. This approach, combined with the talent of Robin van Persie, turned things around for him, and his team were in third position at the end of the season.

There's a strong parallel between the team in sport and the team in business, but there are also some key differences. Professor Sondhi sums up these discrepancies:

Sports teams are smaller than the groupings you find in business. They also produce a measurable output (or fail to do so) every time they play a match, so there is an enormous focus on delivery of results. Businesses could benefit from structuring teams into smaller units. In many cases, teams in business essentially operate as vehicles for distributing workloads. In addition, the key performance measures are not as clearly defined for individuals and teams in the corporate world as they are in football. Measures can be vague and general, leading to inconsistent performance and a lack of clarity in team objectives. Quantification of outcomes is essential in sport, which is why sports science has evolved so that various aspects of the game can be measured: number of shots at goal, number of kilometres run in a game, and so on. Prozone, the leading match-analysis company, for example, measures data related to physical performance and work rates, including distances covered by players and energy expenditure. The analysis can be extremely specific, tailored to answer questions such as, 'How many times did Steven Gerard sprint at over 30 kilometres per hour during the first 45 minutes of the game, in the opposition's half of the field?'

Businesses could benefit from structuring teams into smaller units

A common concern in any team, whether in sport or business, is the need for leaders to be consistent in their behaviour and in the values they promote. Leaders need to be genuine, authentic and true to themselves, consistently, otherwise the human reaction is the same – team members disassociate themselves from the leader. There is an apt saying in this regard: 'Be more concerned with your character than your reputation, because your character is what you really are, but your reputation is merely what people believe you are.' Your character is composed of internal features – personality traits and your value system – whereas your reputation is merely external judgement. The aim, of course, is to ensure that there is no gap between character and reputation, so that you are what you appear to be.

> *A common concern in any team, whether in sport or business, is the need for leaders to be consistent in their behaviour and in the values they promote*

It's not easy to be yourself in the grand soap opera that football has become. Beyond the 90 minutes on the field, where the scrutiny is intense enough, is a thriving industry that has footballers on front pages as well as back, merchandised products from duvet covers to alarm clocks, and constant exposure fuelled by social media and tabloid scandal-mongering. The fans are constantly engaged with their brands (or, as I still like to think of them, the teams they support – I'm a little old-fashioned that way).

This tabloid saturation has fuelled another aspect of the modern football monster: the ego-driven celebrity player. Football may pride itself on its working-class roots and blue-collar heritage, but the days of players emerging from mines or factories to take the field are long gone. The best example from recent times is Carlos Tévez at Manchester City. He is a sublimely gifted footballer and an enormous asset to the game, but the Argentinean striker's fall-out with Roberto Mancini, his manager, proved a major distraction at City. It brought sharply into focus the challenge of managing high-profile footballers who are paid small fortunes and are competing with other players for the 11 spots in the starting side.

Later in the book, we'll look at how Sir Alex has managed the atmosphere in the dressing room, but for now I'll stress the simple point that managing the egos and personalities of a squad of young, wealthy, ambitious footballers, who all believe they should be starting every game, makes for a major management challenge. Balancing a squad is nothing new, certainly, but when an unhappy player knows he can vent his frustration through the tabloids, in an interview, or to half a million followers on Twitter, the manager's lot doesn't get any easier.

Parallel to dealing with difficult individuals, a manager has to maintain contentment in the squad: it is crucial to remain firm, make tough decisions and retain authority while keeping the support and loyalty of the players as individuals and as a group. And this must all be done under relentless public scrutiny, which so ruthlessly raises the level of expectation of teams, players and managers, and in turn dramatically shortens the lifespan of managers in particular. Add in the financial penalties of not making the Champions League, qualifying for the Europa League, or staying in the Premiership, La Liga or Serie A, for example, and no manager ever has true job security. Even Sir Alex hasn't been immune to this; nor have the more established of his contemporaries, including Arsène Wenger. At some point they are all subjected to the daily round of media speculation and gossip.

In short, then, football managers live life in the crosshairs of a trigger-happy firing squad. In that context, it seems almost churlish to describe facing a penalty as a pressurising situation. It's tense, certainly, but even if you pull off the save, there are still 10 other players who can make a crucial mistake or do something silly for which the manager ultimately carries the can.

> *Football managers live life in the crosshairs of a trigger-happy firing squad*

This isn't a heartfelt plea for football managers to be afforded greater leniency. Firstly, that just won't happen; secondly, the men who take those jobs know what lies ahead. For nearly all of them, it's a matter of *when* they'll be fired, not *if*, and they understand that. They know that the media, fans and club owners are poised to pounce at the first sign of frailty. But the managers understand equally that leading one of the big professional teams is a unique opportunity to succeed at the game's highest level, and to create a football legacy. And for all the pressure on them, the pay is not too bad ...

Successful managers are those who deal with the pressure, channel it into effective leadership and emerge with winning teams. Some do it in brief bursts and move on, like José Mourinho

> *Successful managers are those who deal with the pressure, channel it into effective leadership and emerge with winning teams*

(although he's far from football management's first gypsy). Ron Atkinson, who was manager at Manchester United for a good chunk of time, managed Kettering, Cambridge, West Bromwich Albion, Atlético Madrid, Aston Villa, Coventry, Sheffield Wednesday and Nottingham Forest in roughly the same amount of time that Sir Alex has been at United. Harry Redknapp, Graeme Souness and, more recently, Mark Hughes have also been particularly itinerant managers, but while they've all had some degree of success, they've ultimately fallen victim to the uncompromising expectations of owners and fans. Some, like Wenger, hang on for an unusually long spell at a single club, even if the trophies haven't accrued in the desired volume. But no manager has pulled off the sustained period of leadership that Sir Alex Ferguson can lay claim to, where his winning percentage of almost 60 per cent of all matches played since he took over reflects remarkable consistency. (His 459 games at Aberdeen produced a near-identical win rate.)

My own appreciation of pressure has been enhanced considerably not only by observing, understanding and learning from Sir Alex and from football management in general – and from playing under Sir Alex and Sir Bobby – but also from my early days as a professional footballer. It wasn't a case of gradually getting used to performing under pressure; rather it was a case of being thrown in at the deep end – rather like going from junior manager to CEO overnight.

I was a pimply, skinny, cocky teenager who played in the reserves at Manchester United and harboured the outrageous dream of becoming a top-class footballer. The guys I knew were solid working-class lads, and few if any attractive women ever glanced my way. Then, after my debut against Ipswich – a 2-0 win – I was suddenly the toast of the town (well, the red part of it). After dealing with numerous post-match interviews, I met up with my mates in a pub in downtown Manchester. A drink and many a backslap were waiting for me from my mates, but as other United fans recognised me, the scene turned mad, as they all wanted my autograph. Then some Manchester City fans started to call me unpleasant and rather unflattering names, and next thing I knew a fight had started. Brave as a lion, I hit the floor and leopard-crawled out to safety.

The following Monday, my then manager, Dave Sexton, called

me into his office. He wanted to know why I'd wrecked the pub –
he had a huge bill on his desk for damages. I tried my best to
explain that I had had nothing to do with it. Then he told me the
following: I was no longer to hang out with working-class folk,
because I was now a football star, and that would cause problems;
my Wits Engineering T-shirt, with its image of an extended middle
finger, was not appropriate; and my six-wheeler van (which I had
been preparing for a trip around Europe if my stay at United ended)
was never to be seen in the United car park again.

He then gave me a massive cheque and told me to go out and
buy a fancy car, then to get kitted out at a certain clothing shop.
One brand-new, top-of-the-range Alfa Romeo sports car (big in
those days!) and four Armani suits later, and I was a changed man.
Now *that* is as sudden and extreme an introduction to fame as you
can get … and with it came a whole lot of pressure.

My appreciation of pressure has also been enhanced by watching and commentating on 20 years of professional football. You'll
recall the fate of English commentators Andy Gray and Richard
Keys. They were institutions in the coverage of British football,
but lost their jobs after sexist comments were made off-air but
overheard and reported by TV staff in January 2011. Similarly, Ron
Atkinson dealt with a maelstrom of abuse after a racist observation,
also made off-air, was captured by the microphones and carried
onto the airwaves in April 2004.

This was a shame, as I never heard Ron being racist ever, and, in
fact, he was one of the first managers to select black players – the
West Bromwich team of 1978 included Cyrille Regis, Laurie Cun-
ningham and Brendon Batson. The comments made by these
men cannot be condoned, and all three were rightfully taken to
task. Yet these instances do illustrate just how quickly anything
said on air can turn into a news story. Going live on television to

millions of viewers across Africa a couple of times a week, I have to offset my passion for the game and depth of feeling with the knowledge that I need to provide an objective, balanced perspective that falls within accepted broadcasting standards. Much as I might feel the urge to vent my thoughts on a wasteful striker or woeful refereeing, I have to be careful what I say.

This extends to the talks I give on leadership to companies and business leaders. The first time I gave a speech, I was just back from Manchester United and a friend of mine had asked me to give a talk. All I was doing was speaking while I ran through a collection of slides – hardly challenging. But despite having played in front of thousands of people, appeared in cup finals and faced up to some of the deadliest strikers in Europe, I was terrified. I didn't sleep for days beforehand, and I was convinced that half of the audience would walk out.

But I got through it, everyone enjoyed the experience (except me), and 22 years later, speaking publicly is something I do for a living. Is this the same pressure that managers face each week? It's important to understand that pressure comes in different forms, as Professor Sondhi has noted, and that learning to deal with something as minor as talking to a few dozen people can be as important and as challenging as managing a football team.

> *Pressure comes in different forms, and learning to deal with something as minor as talking to a few dozen people can be as important and as challenging as managing a football team*

A large part of overcoming the challenge of public speaking was transforming the pressure I experienced from a negative to a positive. I learnt to appreciate that the audience was there to listen to me, wanted to be there and simply desired the chance to share in some of my experiences. I managed the pressure, and it worked – and Professor Sondhi explains just why this is so important:

A key to managing pressure is to use it as a powerful energiser rather than a destroyer. This can be achieved in the reframing of pressurising situations by incorporating positive-psychology techniques. Reframing involves looking at situations from a different perspective. It becomes easier and more effective when the individual starts to consider why he or she thinks in a particular way. The way we perceive situations, especially when from a negative perspective, adds to the stress we feel. The individual therefore needs to be aware of negative thoughts creeping into the psyche and understand why such thinking is taking place.

> *A key to managing pressure is to use it as a powerful energiser rather than a destroyer*

The next step is to challenge that line of thinking and, as a result, engineer a change in perspective. The final stage of the process is to reframe these negative thoughts as positive thoughts. Some might say this is easier said than done, and they'd be right – it's rarely a simple process. But it becomes easier when we adopt a more positive view of life as a whole, which can be done by expressing gratitude and appreciation for the things we have, rather than showing regret for that which we do not have.

In 1985 I learnt about the power of reframing a difficult situation. I was invited to dinner with a group of Manchester United fans who were attending a high-powered insurance conference. They were dressed in suits, but they would have been right at home on the terraces – a reminder that football has a broad spectrum of fans. (I've often thought about what a top businessman's employees might think if shown a video of their boss hurling abuse at a referee – or goalkeeper – from the stands. Football brings out a very different side to people.) As is usually the case when encountering fans of the club, there were plenty of questions, and with the usual questions came the usual answers, well-honed responses to the standard interrogative. The sports cliché runs thick and fast when professional players are required to give an opinion – 'We're giving 110 per cent', 'The spirit in the camp is good', 'The team that wants it most will win', and so on. It is mundane fare, and I'm afraid I was also guilty of dishing it out. (Now that I'm a television pundit, of course, all of my opinions are unique, insightful and carefully considered ...)

But for once, the ubiquitous answer didn't satisfy the question, and I learnt a great deal as a result. One of the businessmen asked me how I felt when I was in goal for a big game. I responded without thinking, with a reply that was perfectly reasonable but wasn't entirely to the point: 'I'm so honoured to wear the Manchester United badge, and really love playing at the awesome Old Trafford stadium, and—' He stopped me right there: 'No, Gary, I want to know how you *actually* feel!'

I paused, and thought about what the businessman was asking. I focused on how I really did feel when I lined up for a crucial game, knowing that the emotions of 60 000 fans in the ground and millions more around the world would rise and fall with the fortunes of the team and, more importantly for me, with my performance. Eventually, I could only tell him the truth. 'I'm scared to make a mistake,' I admitted. 'If I make a mistake, then the players, manager, crowd and media are on my back, and they make my life hell.' The response from my new philosophical acquaintance was simple. 'In that case, you'll never reach your full potential,' he explained.

'You have to want to be there for your body to respond to its fullest capacity.'

It took a while for the meaning of those words to sink in, but it was the perfect summary of how to face up to a particularly tough challenge. When I started the new season a few weeks later, I was a changed man. I ran onto the pitch willing the opposition to shoot, to test me, to do their best to get past me, so that I could show them just how tough I was going to be to beat. The result? We won our first 10 games of the season, we won the FA Cup in 1985, I was chosen to play for England and I went to the World Cup in Mexico in 1986. All of this was the consequence of changing my attitude from one of fear to one of appreciation for being given the chance to show what I could do.

I'm not the last goalkeeper to have learnt that particular lesson. When Pep Guardiola became coach of Barcelona in 2008, Victor Valdés was established as the club's keeper. But his new coach wasn't happy with him, and explained to Valdés that he didn't just want good players; he wanted players who actually enjoyed the game they were playing. As Valdés himself recalls, Guardiola told him, 'If you go on like this, eventually your career will be over and you won't have enjoyed this wonderful job for a single day because you're always so tense, because success is the only thing you want.' Valdés was a changed man after that: 'He taught me to lower the intensity during a game and coldly analyse what was going on, and to welcome the challenge rather than just lurk there with grim resolution,' the player said.

Not only is change inevitable, but it is a positive force that we need in order to improve

Victor Valdés and I both discovered an invaluable truth: not only is change inevitable, but it is a positive force that we need in order to improve.

The world around us changes, we learnt, and we'll only get left behind if we don't respond in kind and reframe our challenges. Only if you genuinely want to adapt, improve yourself and push on beyond your current comfort zone will you fully deliver on the potential that you have. This philosophy is vital: If you're to succeed under pressure, you have to make a lot of changes, and the most important ones are those that you make within yourself. The professor adds some theory to these practical examples:

Reframing involves seeing a situation from a different perspective, or shifting the focus of what people are paying attention to. A simple key to reframing is to use different concepts and words to explain a situation. You could try to view a problem as an opportunity and a weakness as a strength, for example. The leader, in particular, needs to be able to see a problem and its solution from a fresh perspective. You may have people in the workplace who do not get on with each other – the focus will be on their differences. Reframing would steer clear of their differences and instead focus on their similarities and the things that they have in common. Reframing thus harnesses creative and innovative thinking to achieve breakthrough solutions. When there is a problem, ask yourself: What is the opportunity?

Take the story of Tom Watson when he was in charge of IBM. One of his salespeople made a huge mistake that cost the company $10 million. The person responsible for the error was asked to meet with Watson in his office. He was expecting to be fired and was all ready to leave. Instead, Watson looked at him and said, 'I am not letting you go, having just spent $10 million on your

Reframing harnesses creative and innovative thinking to achieve breakthrough solutions

training.' Watson understood that the mistake had been made and the money was lost. He decided to see the situation as an opportunity rather than as a problem.

At the beginning of my speaking career I felt an enormous pressure to entertain and mesmerise the audience with my stories and message. I was being paid, I thought, so I had to be incredibly good to justify my appearance. But that expectation is nearly impossible to live up to – I was always looking for confirmation from the client after my talk that they were satisfied and that I had rocked their world. Needless to say, that was rarely the case. Then I created a new talk and was advised to ask a top-class speaker to help me. Dr Graeme Codrington turned out to be incredibly helpful, and inspirational too, because when I went to watch him speak, I saw that he was experiencing little or no stress. He was happy to have the opportunity to help people learn from him, and he did so with no ego. Every talk for him was a pleasure, and something he looked forward to.

That is now my approach, and you wouldn't believe the difference. I now stand off-stage, knowing that there are 700 people in the audience, and am excited to go out there and help them all improve their lives and succeed under pressure. The power is now in my hands.

So how does this affect you in the business environment? Are you losing a star employee? You have the chance to develop someone even better. Product sales stalling? This is an opportunity to turn the situation around and create a success story. The competition's launched a new brand? It's your time to go one better. Ultimately it's up to you to reframe the situation to help you cope with the pressure and succeed.

Another incredibly powerful tool is to be grateful for all the positive things you have in your life. Earlier Professor Sondhi mentioned gratitude. By expressing gratitude and appreciation for the things we have, he said, we are able to adopt a more positive outlook on life, as gratitude encompasses appreciation, acceptance and satisfaction. Essentially, gratitude helps to reframe the negative as the positive. In appreciating what you have rather than dwelling on the negative, you begin a snowball effect – yet more recognition of the things that are right in your life is produced, which contributes to your positivity and, ultimately, your success.

By expressing gratitude and appreciation for the things we have, we are able to adopt a more positive outlook on life, as gratitude encompasses appreciation, acceptance and satisfaction

Let me be specific here: I believe that the strongest energy we can attain in our daily lives is from gratitude – it can be of a religious or spiritual nature, or it can come from just being plain thankful. My sense of the world today is that we generally look for problems and rarely focus on the good.

If you are healthy, it's a gift – so be grateful every morning that you wake up in good health. We all know what it feels like to be sick – you haven't got the energy to do anything, the pain is driving you mad, your head feels like it's going to explode. But when the better days come, you usually don't appreciate them fully. My eldest daughter Lara watched her 19-year-old friend fade with cancer over a two-year period, and then die after such agony. I couldn't go to the funeral because I would have been an emotional wreck thinking that it could have been Lara. I have no idea how parents cope with the loss of a child. So every time I see my kids, I'm grateful for my time with them and that they are healthy.

What about your working life? Even if your job is tough, or boring, or driving you up the wall, you can still be grateful for it while you start to figure out whether you can change jobs or re-skill yourself. While you are taking home money, try to remember that there are so many people who don't have a formal job – and will never have the contacts, resources or skills to get one. They will live hand to mouth every day of their lives.

Similarly, consider the Zimbabwean refugees in South Africa, whose number is apparently in excess of 500 000. I took my kids last year to a haven for these refugees to see if we could help with food or any other support. An average-size church in downtown Johannesburg was home to about 6 000 refugees – that's the equivalent of over 100 people living in a semi-detached house in the U.K. Not only was their existence in Johannesburg incredibly tough, but they had left a war-torn country, they'd crossed dangerous rivers to get to South Africa, and many of the women had been raped as they'd entered the country. My kids were shocked by the deprivation, but were made intensely grateful for their own lifestyle, and – even more importantly for me – they all committed to continue helping those in need.

So be grateful. Try to find just one new thing for which to be grateful for every morning. To get yourself in the habit, think of the positive things that you appreciate throughout the day, even if they are as simple as the sun shining, the flowers outside or your kids playing. I guarantee that you will be able to cope with pressure much better through gratitude. Gratitude and unhappiness don't co-exist easily, as gratitude almost always leads to

> *Try to find just one new thing for which to be grateful for every morning*

acceptance and harmony in life, which, in turn, contributes towards a more positive outlook.

Gratitude should inspire the individual to move beyond the ego and stop considering future needs to concentrate on the now: you or your company should be the focus. I love the mantra, 'Comparison is the thief of joy.' Evolutionary theory suggests that we compare ourselves to people who have more than us in excess of 66 per cent of the time to improve and increase our chances of survival. This leads to our feeling less than positive and always wanting more. While it is necessary to be aware of competition and other people's achievements, don't let them dictate or lessen your appreciation for the positive in your own life. In fact, you need to be more grateful on a regular basis during the day just to balance the effects of always comparing up!

While it is necessary to be aware of competition and other people's achievements, don't let them dictate or lessen your appreciation for the positive in your own life

Older football fans will re-member Norman Whiteside, a hard, uncompromising mid-fielder who might have been Northern Ireland's greatest ever footballing export were it not for a long-haired genius called George Best. There was a simple but established hierarchy in the Manchester United dressing room. Younger play-ers would come in to clean our boots, pick up menial tasks and get a feel for the first-team environment. Whiteside had arrived as a six-foot-tall, 13-year-old skinhead from the Shankill Road area of Belfast, the centre of what Ulstermen look back on euphe-mistically as 'the Troubles'. Even then, he cut an imposing figure.

And he did so particularly when, on one of his first visits to the dressing room, I casually instructed him to ask the broom in the corner for a dance, as part of our fun initiation procedure. Usually, the youngster would obey the instruction and we'd all shout, 'Get lost, you ugly bastard,' or words to that effect, but Whiteside responded in the manner of Wayne Rooney getting a yellow card … in other words, he told me to get lost in a considerably less than pleasant manner. I tried again, and got the same response, only more vigorous. Thankfully the call came for us to go out onto the field just then, and a potentially awkward situation was defused.

In 1982, when he became the youngest player (at 16) ever to play in the World Cup finals, I asked Whiteside about the incident. He explained that he had grown up in an area where bombs went off every week, Protestants and Catholics fought daily, and life was lived in a climate of fear and antagonism. After that, he said, a smiling blond South African with a university degree and a habit of using moisturiser was hardly going to scare him. This made me realise how fortunate an upbringing I'd had, having lived in an upper-class suburb in Cape Town and attended one of the top schools in the area.

Fast-forward to the end of my time at United, when another unexpected lesson in perspective occurred. When Sir Alex and I agreed that the prognosis on my knee was not good and that retirement from professional football was the best option, I was asked to see the England doctor, Dr John Crane, who was also the Arsenal doctor. I needed to finalise things from an administrative point of view – I'd been injured on England duty, which would influence my retirement payment. I met Dr Crane after the game against Watford in late April 1987, and he took me through to the physiotherapist's room, put me on the table and checked the movement of my knee. The doctor looked at the specialist's report and agreed that this was the end of the road for me. Seeing my deep disappointment, which I obviously hadn't been hiding as well as I'd thought, he said that it must be tough. He then excused himself for a moment, and came back a few minutes later, saying that he wanted to introduce me to the young lad getting treatment in the next room.

I met the kid, and we chatted about his injuries and about football. Afterwards Dr Crane took me back to the original room and revealed that the 17-year-old boy I'd been talking to had been tackled so badly that both of his knees were a wreck. The doctor was just hoping that the boy would walk properly soon, never mind play football professionally. He then told me how lucky I was to have played nearly 400 times for the biggest club in the world, been keeper for England and gone to a World Cup. I needed to look on the bright side, he said.

This incident played a major role in helping me to get over my despair and move into a space where I was able to start considering a new, post-football career. Looking at a situation through a 'grateful lens' is one of the most powerful ways to get through difficult times.

> *Looking at a situation through a 'grateful lens' is one of the most powerful ways to get through difficult times*

I remember both of those events for the enduring lessons they taught me in appreciating my circumstances and being grateful for what I have. Appreciation and gratitude facilitate a sense of awareness and perspective that is absolutely vital in achieving success in your chosen field. There'll be other examples of similar lessons learnt as this book unfolds, but being stood up to in my own first-team dressing room by a fearless 13-year-old raised in a war-torn territory, and seeing a talented 17-year-old lose his career before it had even started, remain two of the most vivid.

Research has shown that people who are grateful are 25 per cent happier.* These people also tend be more optimistic and to exercise more frequently. Interestingly, the same research revealed that the things people are most grateful for are the smaller things in life – a sunny day, for instance. Another interesting finding was that gratitude should take the form of true gratefulness rather than comparative gratefulness, which involves merely feeling that you are happier than someone else. Since gratitude provides for a more positive mindset and a happier existence, the link between gratitude and reframing is crucial. By finding things to be grateful for, an individual is likely to be happier, more functional and, ultimately, more successful.

In any performance-related environment, people are happier when they regularly set themselves challenges. Since happiness is affected by a higher frequency of positive experiences rather than by the intensity of positive experiences, these challenges need to comprise smaller targets, which allow for an increased number of positive experiences: when individuals hit big targets, the impact wears off just as quickly as it would for smaller targets. As more targets are hit, happiness becomes more deeply ingrained in the personality of the individual.

> *In any performance-related environment, people are happier when they regularly set themselves challenges*

Psychologist Professor Sonja Lyubomirsky and colleagues have

---

* R.A. Emmons and M.E. McCullough, 'Counting blessings versus burdens: An experimental investigation of gratitude and subjective well-being in daily life', *Journal of Personality and Social Psychology* 84 (2), 2003, pp. 377–389.

pointed out that there is plenty of evidence to suggest that happiness can lead to success.** They have also stated that success is a moving target: once you hit the target, people will raise the bar. These studies show that happy people are more likely to talk to others, be interested in and enjoy leisure activities, enjoy social interactions, resolve conflicts effectively, help others, feel healthier, be more creative, perform complex tasks better and confidently attribute success to their own skills.

Since our brains are highly adaptable, we are able to change our attitudes. For many years people assumed that our brains deteriorated as we got older; however, the field of neuroplasticity has shown that though the number of neurons in the brain might decrease as we age, the connections between these neurons (our experiences and knowledge) actually have no limits. They continue to grow as we get older, which means that we are all capable of change. We do, however, have to work harder as we get older.

You can improve your happiness by doing simple things each day, such as writing down three things for which you are grateful, meditating for five minutes, exercising for at least 20 minutes or writing a journal of meaningful experiences. The specific task isn't as important as the process behind it: reminding yourself of the good things in life, and thus carrying that positive thought process into everything else that you do, helps with self-reflection and learning. Generally, it takes around 30 days of action (on a regular basis) to create new habits. These habits will enhance your appreciation of life and your happiness, and this will help you to succeed under pressure.

** S. Lyubomirsky, L. King and E. Diener, 'The benefits of frequent positive affect: Does happiness lead to success?', *Psychological Bulletin* 131, 2005, pp. 803–855.

Gratitude and happiness, key ingredients in the personality of the individual, are essential to ensuring that the implementation of the LEADS framework is effective. As already discussed, success under pressure is based on this framework, which contains the five key ingredients we have identified in the most successful people in football. Research into the business world verifies that these ingredients are as valid as in the sporting arena.

Another way in which pressure can be relieved is through humour. I always say that the best humour comes from the U.K., because living in that climate means you have to find something to laugh about. Humour helps to reduce the pressure. My dad, who was English, was a big one for laughs and pranks, and when I was at United we were at it all the time. After my debut I had to speak to the cameras straight after the game and go and see the chairman, Louis Edwards. Just before doing so, all the players were congratulating me in the dressing room, saying what a perfect debut it had been. I thought I was surrounded by love and care – until I started to put on my socks and found that they'd been cut in half. What was left didn't even cover my toes. When I asked about it, no one owned up; my teammates all smirked and said that someone was being really silly. When I went to put on my tie, I found that all that was left was enough to make a bowtie. That's when everyone around me collapsed in laughter. It certainly took the tension out of meeting the media and the chairman.

Humour helps to reduce the pressure

My dad was always one for tricks, but he got caught out by two former West Bromwich Albion stars, Cyrille Regis and Gary Owen. My dad was taking them around South Africa on a coaching course in the early 1980s. He would play silly tricks on them, like putting salt in their ice cream and chilli on their knives and forks. Then they got their revenge. He had said that he was going to his room for a quick shower. They waited outside his room for five minutes before knocking on the door. When he opened it, with just a towel round his waist, they said Cyrille had cut his leg badly and would have to go to hospital. As Cyrille moved to show him the 'cut', Gary grabbed my dad's towel and slammed his door shut. The two of them ran down the stairs, leaving my dad stranded in the corridor with no clothes, no key and the very embarrassing challenge of getting help from those exiting the lift on his floor – without being accused of being a pervert, or worse. Needless to say, both Cyrille and Gary slept with their eyes open for the rest of the trip.

If you want a good night's sleep, avoid travelling on a plane with a sports team, especially if it's a long-haul flight. Imagine a 30-hour journey to Brisbane from Manchester. I was desperately tired after playing a game and watching movies. While I was sleeping, one of my teammates balanced a polystyrene cup full of water gently on my head before scampering back to his seat. Somebody shouted out my name and I woke with a start, only to feel the cup tip and drench me with water. I never found out who was responsible, but this incident, and pranks like it, helped to ease the boredom that often increases the pressure while on tour.

Humour, however silly, is not the only way to reduce pressure. One of the most surprising techniques comes from my former manager, who is constantly under intense pressure. In recent years, Sir Alex Ferguson has taken up gardening, not to help out the groundsmen at Old Trafford after Nemanja Vidić and Rio Ferdinand have spent an afternoon taking chunks out of the pitch, but as a calming distraction from the world of football. Sir Alex carefully tending to his petunias is not an image that comes easily to mind, but it illustrates the adaptive nature of a man who recognises the need for a balanced environment. This balance allows him not just to succeed, but to thrive under pressure.

Professor Sondhi expands on how the game has changed for the modern football manager, and why it serves up such a rich lesson in dealing with pressure:

Football, and in particular Premiership football in England, has seen massive changes in the past 20 years. Huge investment has been made in the league, and also in specific clubs. The need to succeed has increased as wealthy owners demand success, whatever the cost. The globalisation of the sport has created an enormous influx of players from different cultures and different parts of the world. This has given rise to a dynamic environment characterised by uncertainty, which has demanded an unprecedented adaptability from football leadership.

It's not just football managers and players who are feeling increased pressure to succeed, however. The business world has seen pressure increase tremendously since the recession, with no sign of it abating. Profits are down, margins are being squeezed, jobs are being lost and the markets are uncertain at best. For me there is no question that everyone in business is feeling the pressure, which is why there is a growing need to deal with it in a manner that brings you the success you want and makes it fun in the process.

THE TRAINING SESSION

To help develop the skills for coping with pressure, here are a few tasks that will help you to cement the concepts discussed in this chapter:

1. List situations in which you feel pressured. What other people were involved in the situation? What is your attitude towards

them? Do you hold them in high esteem? Are you afraid of them? What are the expectations of these people? What are your internal emotions towards these groups of people?

2. List three to five things that you are most grateful for, and state why.

3. Examine the circumstances in your life that you perceive to be negative and reframe them from the perspective of an optimist.

FULL-TIME TAKEAWAY

- Pressure is based on expectations that are often imposed by us, so reframe your situation to make it more exciting and relevant – this will relieve some of the pressure and change your physical response to the situation.
- Make being grateful a habit, especially first thing in the morning and last thing at night. Try to extend this to every opportunity during the day.
- Businesses can benefit from structuring themselves into productive teams of smaller numbers, like a football team, with clear and measurable objectives.
- Use humour to lighten the moment and relieve the pressure.

2

Leadership

'Great leadership is never built without
having the humility and honest desire
to learn from everybody around you.'
– *Ken Allen, CEO of DHL Express*

When Alex Ferguson first walked into our dressing room way back
in November 1986, all the Manchester United players were wondering what was so special about the man who, in a league entirely
dominated by Rangers and Celtic, had brought such spectacular
success to Aberdeen – hardly a giant of Scottish football, let alone
European football. More importantly, we were wondering if this
was going to be the man to guide us to winning the First Division
championship (as it was then) for the first time since 1967. As a
senior player, I was keenly aware of just how important it was for
Ferguson to bring success to Manchester United after decades without winning the league championship.

United's fans, while unquestionably faithful, are to this day a passionate, knowledgeable collective who expect a return on that faith, and are happy to make it known when they feel they're being sold short. Try standing in goal with the home crowd at your back after a run of defeats and you'll know exactly what I mean.

There was enormous pressure on the man who replaced Ron Atkinson, and we were all unsure of how a Scottish manager we didn't know much about would handle one of the most demanding jobs in sport. (That was in 1986; 25 years on, and the pressure is even greater.) Had you told us then what Sir Alex would go on to achieve at Old Trafford, we'd have smiled politely and bought you another drink.

In those first days and weeks of the Ferguson era, though, I began to understand that the new manager was something special. His qualities as a leader quickly became apparent, and it's exactly those qualities that tie in with the first part of the LEADS acronym: leadership.

Of the many books I've read on leadership (a slow process, as a footballer), *Good to Great* by Jim Collins stands out. If you haven't read it, here's the truncated version: Collins and his team identified and researched about 1500 Fortune 500 companies with the goal of working out who stood out in terms of commercial success, and why. The 1500 were narrowed down to 11 companies that had for 15 years or more outperformed the stock market. Key to every one of these companies was strong, effective leadership.

The two factors that emerged from Collins's study as key to leadership were professional will and personal humility: in tandem, they produced what Collins referred to as 'level-five leadership'. When I first read *Good to Great* – something I've done many times since – I kept coming back to the same parallel: the leadership qualities being discussed by one of the business world's foremost academics were all applicable to my old manager.

Let me start with personal humility, seen by Collins as the ability of a leader to remove him- or herself from revelling in success and, instead, to pass on the kudos to the rest of the team. Humility reflects a willingness to understand yourself as an individual (your identity, strengths and limitations), and to combine that understanding with a complete perspective on your relationships with others. Cue the perfect example ... The morning after Manchester United had won the historic treble of Premier League, FA Cup and Champions League in 1999, I bumped into Sir Alex in the corridors of Old Trafford. By rights he should have been surrounded by champagne and cigar smoke, cheerfully accepting the praise being heaped upon him.

'You're the greatest, the best ever!' I gushed when I saw him, overawed at the magnitude of what United had just achieved. But Sir Alex's reply immediately illustrated the perspective he has always had. 'Gary, this is not about me,' he smiled in response. 'It's about the players. Weren't they magnificent last night?'

When you contrast such humble behaviour with the brash, self-conscious leadership of José Mourinho, for example, whose tenures as coach have been fleeting compared to Ferguson's, you begin to understand the value of humility in leadership.

I learnt about humility and gratitude when I arrived in Manchester from South Africa as a 19-year-old goalkeeping hopeful and went from unsigned nobody to Manchester United goalkeeper. I might have been high on professional will (I'd played a thousand games for United in my back garden, at school and in deep, smiling sleep, always saving the crucial penalty to win the FA Cup), but trying to stay humble as a teenager elevated to the starting XI of the world's greatest football teams is nigh on impossible. I'd achieved early success, the fans seemed to have taken to me and the press was positive. I was also educated, having studied at Wits University, whereas most players in this decidedly blue-collar sport had at best finished high school. Subconsciously, that added to an already simmering arrogance – all of which set me up for the fall my career needed.

It was the 1979 FA Cup final against Arsenal. Not yet 21, I was starting in English football's marquee game after only four months in the first team, and I think I was the youngest keeper to have played in an FA Cup final. I floated down the tunnel and onto the pitch, deliriously happy. My high spirits didn't last. With the entire planet watching the biggest moment of my life – 90 minutes that would surely end with me lifting a winner's medal after a man-of-the-match performance – we were 2-0 down by half-time. That's how it stayed until, with five minutes to go – and this was voted the greatest ending ever to any cup final – we pulled one back, giving our supporters a shred of hope. And then, incredibly, we scored another, levelling the game. It would surely send us into extra time. It was at this point that I discovered for the first time just how truly cruel the beautiful game can be.

The moment, much as I've tried to erase it from a stubbornly clear memory, still plays out in slow motion. From the kick-off after our equaliser, Arsenal played it wide, the cross came in and the 20-year-old superstar, the hottest property in the history of keeping, couldn't reach it. Alan Sunderland scored, the final whistle went (not that I heard it), and Manchester United had lost the FA Cup final. Thanks to Gary Bailey.

It's generally the goalkeepers who cop the blame when something goes wrong in defence – ask Iker Casillas, Joe Hart, Robert Green or Peter Shilton, and they'll all tell you, quite objectively, that keepers should be paid double that which strikers get for wandering round the 18-yard area, with the very occasional burst of real work. But whether you deserve it or not (and in this case I certainly wasn't without fault), you can't escape it: I spent the next four weeks dealing with a barrage of abuse from the press, disillusioned fans, taxi drivers – the list goes on.

It was my dad who yanked me out of my self-pity and got me to appreciate just how much I could take out of that defeat. He'd played for 10 years for Ipswich and Crystal Palace and had never featured in an FA Cup final; in fact, he'd never even got as far as a quarter-final. And yet, at just 20, I'd already had an opportunity most professional players in England had never experienced, my own father being one of them. I'd been taught a salient lesson in humility and gratitude, one that still serves me to this day (in that enduring memory of 1979).

It also firmed up my professional will: that experience only drove me harder, causing me to cherish subsequent FA Cup success all the more. In short, while I didn't leave Wembley with a winner's medal, I did gain invaluable lessons in personal leadership. Sometimes taking a knock is the best thing that can happen to you – as long as you learn from it and come back stronger (although carrying the can for losing one FA Cup final is quite enough, thank you).

Sometimes taking a knock is the best thing that can happen to you – as long as you learn from it and come back stronger

Humility extends to a willingness to learn from the advice and opinions of others. When injury brought my career in England to a premature end in 1987, Sir Alex called me into his office and asked me what I thought he should be doing to create long-term success at Old Trafford. He is not seen as the kind of manager who

61

would canvass the opinions of his former players, particularly given the legendary 'hairdryer' he brings out at half-time, yet here he was, asking me what I thought he needed to do. That's not a sign of weakness. Rather, it's a considerable strength. In recognising the value of others' views, Sir Alex has broadened his own vision and emerged a better leader for it. He may not have used the advice I gave that day, but he appreciated and valued it nonetheless, and I felt valued in the process.

Years later, when I had just started giving the talks and presentations that led to writing this book, I found myself speaking in Dubai at a leadership conference. Bearing in mind the audience of over a thousand people and the distinguished list of speakers, I asked one of the other speakers for some advice. He responded by asking me if I really wanted to hear what he thought. When I insisted that I did, he told me that I wasn't an expert in leadership, that it wasn't my area of authority.

Having delivered a bruising blow to my ego, he then said that I was an expert on something else: succeeding under pressure. Playing in goal for Manchester United had given me experience that no one else at the conference could draw from, and *that* was what I should speak about. And so the initial dent in my pride was followed by an objective, honest appraisal that changed my approach to speaking, all because I'd been humble enough to ask someone for some good, honest advice.

Again, look at Mourinho. Can you picture a man who dubs himself 'The Special One' asking for advice, or radically changing his approach based on external criticism, no matter how constructive it might be? I believe that Mourinho is a very good manager, as his record proves, but, like the rest of us, he could learn a few lessons from Sir Alex. Professor Sondhi elaborates on this point:

Gary has shown that humility is not a weakness, but a strength. Self-worth is crucial in that it enables the leader not to feel inhibited in asking for help. This was also demonstrated by Sir Alex in the way he responded to the challenges of working with diverse cultures. Recognising that he was unable to get the best out of Latin players like Juan Sebastián Verón, he brought in Carlos Queiroz (who speaks six languages; seven if you count the form of English spoken in Liverpool!) to help with the management of these players. Not only did this turn things around, but it led to United producing one of the greatest footballers of all time – Cristiano Ronaldo. More importantly for the club, it inspired considerable success: the European Champions League in 2008, and domestic league and cup glory. This element of humility only works, however, if the leader is prepared to carry out a true self-assessment of his or her own strengths and weaknesses.

Self-worth is crucial in that it enables the leader not to feel inhibited in asking for help

The leader that possesses humility focuses on the team and the priorities of the team rather than on the self. Sir Alex has illustrated this on many occasions. One prime example is his dropping of Jim Leighton just before the replay of the 1990 FA Cup final. Manchester United had been lucky to draw the original game against Crystal Palace 3-3. Leighton had had a disastrous match and was feeling the pressure. Before signing him at United, Sir Alex had brought Leighton up from a youngster

The leader that possesses humility focuses on the team and the priorities of the team rather than on the self

at Aberdeen; however, the manager recognised the importance of the replay and brought in Les Sealey in Leighton's place, initially as a short-term replacement, although Sealey did continue the following season. Sir Alex's actions indicate that the team is more important than the emotional ties of the leader to one of his players.

Humility is sometimes oversimplified as the acknowledgement of others. In truth, it is a mindset underpinned by a belief in inter-dependence and an acceptance that the bigger goal cannot be achieved without help from others. Many of the football managers examined in this book are recognised for the strength of their 'back-room teams'. Sir Bobby Robson used to have a member of staff at Barcelona called José Mourinho ... not a bad choice. Sir Alex, too, has relied on loyal and highly effective number twos. He has no problem combining his knowledge with that of other leading think-ers in the game, appearing to recognise that to stay at the top you need to surround yourself with the best – just think of his former number twos, such as Steve McClaren, who went on to manage England; Walter Smith, who was a manager of Everton; and Carlos Queiroz, who managed Portugal in the 2010 World Cup.

Another factor common to leaders who practise humility is that they treat everyone in the same way, whatever their posi-tion. Sir Alex reportedly knows the names of everyone who works for Manchester United and makes a habit of talking to them all. Gary has mentioned to me that other managers he played for hardly knew some of the junior players coming through into the senior squad.

High-performing people tend not to have grandiose percep-

> *Another factor common to leaders who practise humility is that they treat everyone in the same way, whatever their position*

tions of themselves, nor are they self-deprecating – they have a firm sense of self-worth, and confidence in their abilities. There is a danger that humility can be perceived as a weakness, taking the form of low self-esteem and a lack of confidence. In 2012, certain people criticised Sir Alex for bringing back 37-year-old Paul Scholes, the world-class midfielder, saying it was a sign of weakness. Sir Alex's response was interesting. With a total lack of anger, he said, 'If bringing back one of the best midfielders in the world over the last 20 years is a sign of weakness, then we can live with that.' His quiet confidence indicates a strong sense of self-worth and humility.

José Mourinho may be seen as anything but humble. He likes to be known as 'The Special One', which, whether deliberate or not, means that in public the pressure is taken off his team and focused on the manager himself. This may lead to a lack of sustainability of the success he has created at his clubs, however, evidenced by what his former clubs, such as Porto, Chelsea and Inter Milan, have achieved – or failed to achieve – since he left. While they have not been as successful, Mourinho himself has. In short, his coaching style is about Mourinho rather than the club – which is ultimately a limitation. I do wonder, however, if he has now matured and perhaps even learnt from Sir Alex. If I were a betting man, I'd wager that he will, in fact, create a lasting legacy at Real Madrid.

An excellent summary on humility from the professor, but how does humility in the leadership of a football team translate into the business arena? Just as Sir Alex invited me to contribute my opinion to his leadership process, leaders in business can seek the views of others and, in doing so, create an environment in which employees not only feel encouraged to offer their input, but see that their input is being appreciated and often used. Couple that with a willingness to take individual responsibility for failure, and you have a leadership model that promotes loyalty, creativity and a stronger team dynamic.

I was taught many lessons in humility on the football field – let a ball slip through your hands and into the net in a stadium full of vociferous fans, and you know all about it for the rest of the match. But my first real lesson in humility in the business world was the most salient. Recently retired from football, I was in financial strife after several failed investments and an economic downturn in London. To provide a bit of background: I had enjoyed a wonderful testimonial game between Manchester United and England at Old Trafford, and I had also received a large insurance payment for my injury. The best advice I could take up, I thought, was to buy property in London. So, after selling up my house and goods in Manchester, I spent a few weeks with some advisors finding good properties that would yield decent rentals. That was April 1987.

Within months the market had crashed, and I was suddenly under severe financial pressure as the rental rates dropped and interest rates doubled. To make matters worse, I had also bought a holiday home at a game farm two hours north of Johannesburg, something I'd dreamt of doing during my cold and wet days in Manchester. Literally weeks after the property crash in England, this development fell into bankruptcy. Only then did I realise that my 'freehold property' was, in fact, 52 weeks of timeshare – and I was on the verge of losing that too.

It got even worse: the owner of the resort had asked me two months earlier, as a favour, to be a director (it would look good on the letterhead, he said). I was now being threatened with legal suits if it was found that there was any wrongdoing on the part of the company that managed the game reserve. And then came the straw that broke the camel's back: I filed as a concurrent creditor to get money back from the hotel, which had been using my holiday home for spill-over guests on busy nights, only to be told that if the main creditors, who were preferential, didn't get enough money from the bankrupt business, they could approach me to reclaim their money ... essentially, I was owed money but I might have had to pay in!

I was fuming; when I got home after hearing that news I hit the punching bag in my garage until my hands were bleeding. Ten years of earnings from United were gone, all my effort to get a degree while playing had been with the express purpose to avoid such a scenario, and now I was facing possible criminal charges for something that I hadn't even been aware of.

But there was more: the business I had set up after retiring from Kaizer Chiefs involved using workers' passion for football to increase their productivity, but with the trade unions trying to destabilise the apartheid government and deliberately undermining productivity, my business was suddenly coming up against a brick wall.

I knew I needed to find a job in a different field. I had always enjoyed talking to the radio and TV guys when I'd been a player, so I started looking around for whatever work I could get in that field. I had approached a friend of mine, former Lions scrumhalf John Robbie, who at that time was on the rise at Talk Radio 702 in Johannesburg. The initial enquiries he made on my behalf came to nothing, as the radio station had employed someone just a few weeks earlier.

I realised then how humbling it is to go around looking for work and to face constant rejection. What skills did I have? I had a physics degree (99 per cent of which I'd forgotten), football skills (no use outside of football) and a willingness to work hard – and that was it. Those weeks of waiting for a phone call from a place-ment agency were some of my toughest ever. My mind was frantic: What if I didn't get a job? Would I have to go back to university to learn something new? How could I fall so low so quickly when I had put everything in place to prevent this from happening?

Then John called me. The night before, the new sports anchor had been reading the tennis results and had pronounced the name of French player Guy Forget – which is pronounced *Gee Forsjay* – quite literally as 'Guy Forget'. He was out – and I had been given a lifeline.

It was tough – I was getting up at 4.30 a.m. every day to get to the studio, where I was being taught to use basic recording equip-ment by a 20-year-old who couldn't believe how technologically inept I was. So it was a humbling step down from the Old Trafford first team, but it taught me some important lessons that I use today, both in my presentations and in managing my own life. The value of humility is not just in the self-awareness it creates, but also in the understanding it provides leaders with when employed as a leadership tool. It works for United – as Sir Alex has shown – it works for me, and it can work for your business, as Professor Sondhi illustrates:

> *It is imperative to avoid beliefs dictating that we are not good enough in some fundamental way, that we have to do something to earn love, or that we have to be someone we're not in order to be accepted*

To build the qualities of humility, we need to begin by assessing our beliefs. It is imperative to avoid beliefs dictating that we are not good enough in some fundamental way, that we have to do something to earn love, or that we have to be someone we're not in order to be accepted. Our beliefs should focus on the positive factors that build self-confidence, without stimulating over-confidence. We have to believe that we have something to offer in a relationship and that the people we associate with also bring value. This brings with it a desire to learn, which necessarily involves change.

Research has shown that negative perceptions and negative self-judgement are the result of certain thought patterns in the brain. Our brains are neuro-plastic, which means that these patterns can be reprogrammed. Thus neuro-linguistic programming (NLP) may be used to create the new mental patterns, which involves taking specific situations that we would like to change and replaying them in our minds, with a focus on the way we would like to behave.

An ideal example of this can be seen in the cassette tapes I recorded while I was in England. I would play them in my car on the way to and from training (today you could do the same by recording your messages on your mobile phone and listening to them on the train or in the car). On these cassettes I'd run through the positives of being at United, the opportunity I'd been given and the success I could achieve with the right mindset. Constantly driving home my objectives and the path that I needed to take to reach those objectives kept me firmly focused, particularly when I'd had a bad game, was missing home or had simply had enough of yet another week without a glimmer of sunshine. They also kept me grounded – they were a refresher course in humility, if you like.

But humility, Collins explains in *Good to Great*, is only half of the success; the other half lies in professional will, which is vital in offsetting the potential pitfalls of leadership in which the humility factor can become a weakness. It's all well and good to have an inclusive model in play, but if you allow your company to adopt a leadership-by-committee policy, it is likely that you'll be headed towards the sort of bureaucratic process we tend to associate with government. Can you imagine Manchester United team selection as a collective effort, where £100 000-a-week footballers try to sort out who deserves to be in the first XI? Think of chaotic France in the 2010 World Cup, and you have the perfect illustration of why the collective contribution has to be managed by strong leadership.

The professional will that Collins speaks of, then, refers to the sense of ambition and determination that a leader possesses – traits that to a degree seem at odds with humility. Focused, driven and with a certain emotional detachment that allows decisions to be made with as clear a head as possible, the leader with professional will ensures that his or her passion doesn't become an Achilles heel, and that the humility infused into the team plays off against a steely foundation of direction and focus. This is professional will.

One example stands out above all others: David Beckham. The 'new Gary Bailey', as I like to think of Beckham (to the violent disagreement of my daughters, who sadly see their father as a source of pocket money rather than as a heart-throb footballer), is one of the most iconic players of the modern game, and it was Old Trafford that introduced him to the world. Hard-working, committed, a masterful passer of the ball, and possessed of as good a right foot as I've ever seen (I'm happy never to have been on the wrong end of a Beckham free kick), he quickly became the poster boy of the finest generation of home-grown talent from an English club since Matt Busby's ill-fated stars.

But as Beckham grew, so did the Beckham brand: the pop-star wife, the commercial endorsements and the distractions of life beyond the football field. Sir Alex is the antithesis of all of that –

picturing him endorsing a washing powder or an Italian fragrance in a television commercial is beyond the scope of my imagination – but he's well aware of what football has become, and that allowing a certain amount of leeway is essential to keep players content.

Beckham went beyond what Sir Alex felt was acceptable, however. He took it to the point where his manager felt the team was suffering because of the star player and his lifestyle, and so, in one of the boldest moves in football, Beckham was sold. It proved commercially shrewd, but it also didn't harm the team: United's record since Beckham's departure is ample proof of that, and a clear illustration of the emotional detachment often required by a good leader, as mentioned earlier.

There are further examples of this – Jaap Stam, Ruud van Nistelrooy and Cristiano Ronaldo are among the high-profile players Ferguson has let go for the good of the team. With Stam, it was for breaking the unwritten rule of criticising the club or manager, as the Dutchman did in his autobiography. Gary Neville writes in his autobiography that Sir Alex stated publicly, 'Jaap is a bit embarrassed by it all. He's very regretful now, and he has some making up to do in the dressing room.' Neville says, however, that 'it seems the United manager dealt with the issue more severely. Stam was the latest big name at United to have a run-in with Sir Alex Ferguson, and he would face the same as those before him, including Paul McGrath, Norman Whiteside and Paul Ince.'

Letting Ronaldo go, however, was a function of accepting that the player wanted to move on, and that keeping him in Manchester against his will simply wasn't going to work. Time and again, players have been replaced, gaps have been filled and the team has proved stronger than the individual, all under the leadership of an astute manager with a strong professional will. 'Alex was prepared to be hard,' Bryan Robson remarked in his autobiography, 'and move players on when he felt it was necessary.' Much as he's been genuinely fond of his players, Sir Alex has kept clear of sentiment when making decisions on buying and selling, and that's a result of his iron will, to which Professor Sondhi pays tribute:

Athletes and performers from all backgrounds possess a degree of will and determination, as these are the drivers of action. There are differing degrees of determination, though, and the level of will is connected to the amount of humility possessed by the individual. If an individual feels that he or she has nothing further to learn, then the level of commitment diminishes. This is certainly not the case for Sir Alex Ferguson.

If an individual feels that he or she has nothing further to learn, then the level of commitment diminishes

After the 2011/12 season, media pundits claimed that the Manchester United team was the worst for a number of years ... yet they finished second, beaten only on goal difference. The repeated suggestion in the media was that the only reason the team got that close to victory was because of one man, Sir Alex Ferguson. It is testament to his leadership that the outcomes of a number of competitive games involving 34 active people (players, substitutes, referees, linesmen and the fourth official) have been attributed to him – a single individual who's not even playing.

So where does all of this slot into business leadership? While you might not be dealing with a David Beckham or Cristiano Ronaldo on a weekly basis, the principles of professional will remain the same. Blending the strengths and offsetting the weaknesses of your team is, at the simplest level, what both football and business management are about.

During the 2001/02 season, Manchester United endured a horror run: they found themselves in 10th position. Mid-table security would suit most sides in a cut-and-thrust league where three or four clubs are genuine contenders and the rest are merely hoping to stay up for another year, with a possible crack at fringe European competition. When you're Manchester United, however, and 10th place is as low as you've been since the Premier League's inception, you've hit the iceberg and the band has started playing. Or, at least, that's how the media gleefully sized up the situation. United were in freefall, the Old Trafford empire was crumbling and Ferguson would be on the dole within weeks.

Four weeks and seven matches later, United were at the top of the league again. Bouncing back so emphatically that season reflects the single-minded determination that has kept Sir Alex at the top of an industry which takes pride in bringing managers to their knees each and every season. It's worth looking at some of the initiatives he has overseen during his time in charge.

Relationships with clubs in South America and Asia, as well as with European clubs, such as Royal Antwerp, aren't merely useful collaborations for commercial gain. (Although Beckham shirts were a massive winner for United in Asia, Gary Bailey–replica goalkeeper jerseys moved in slightly more modest numbers.) Sir Alex has used these links to dig up exciting young players to recruit to the United squad and in the process brought a more global understanding to United's play. His professional will ensured that he brought the world to Old Trafford and he has expertly managed the resultant infusion of international talent.

'What you could certainly recognise in him was that drive, that almost manic desire which I think has played a big part in his success,' comments one of Sir Alex's many biographers. 'I think he's unique in that way ... and he's carried it through his career.' Brian McClair offers a similar assessment of Sir Alex in his auto-biography: 'He is extremely tough mentally, and able to stand up to the repercussions of what he does, and he expects his players to do the same.'

It's not just players that Sir Alex's vision extends to; he has a strong desire to surround himself with the best people at every level. When Brian Kidd decided to leave the assistant-manager job at Old Trafford to take on the head role at Blackburn Rovers, Sir Alex wished him well but took his time to hand-pick a replacement. The man he selected was one of the best: Steve McClaren, who was then at Derby County. McClaren brought an inno-vative edge to United and proved an outstanding lieu-

> *It's not just players that Sir Alex's vision extends to; he has a strong desire to surround himself with the best people at every level*

tenant. (Kidd was sacked from the Blackburn job a year later; McClaren helped United to a treble. The man smiling at the end of it all? Sir Alex.)

In later years he brought in Carlos Queiroz, the Portuguese coach who subsequently endured difficult spells with Bafana Bafana and Real Madrid; at United he was exceptional, and a valuable asset in a team increasingly enjoying the influence of the Latin game.

Picking the right team, having the right people by your side, garnering opinion but making the important decisions yourself, driving your team forward by example: the facets of successful leadership are multiple, and balancing them effectively is as much of a challenge as anything else.

My friend Anton Roux, who heads up Aon Sub-Saharan Africa, offers two great pieces of advice on building a team. The first is as follows: 'Recruit people with the correct attitude, and then provide them with the skill.' Before Sir Alex buys a player, he wants to know whether that player's character will fit in with the club – is he a fighter? Is he ambitious? Is he a team player? If not, he won't sign the player, because he knows that this new man could infect the team with the wrong attitude (Éric Cantona is perhaps one of the very few exceptions to this). The culture you create in a team must be one that brings everyone together in pressurised situations rather than one that alienates or divides them.

> *The facets of successful leadership are multiple, and balancing them effectively is as much of a challenge as anything else*

Anton's second suggestion is to 'organise yourself out of a job – if you don't create spare capacity around yourself, you will never have the ability to do more and to grow'. The successful leader learns to delegate and pass on responsibilities, and in the process frees up time to focus on other areas of the organisation.

> *The successful leader learns to delegate and pass on responsibilities, and in the process frees up time to focus on other areas of the organisation*

Manchester United's manager might not be universally popular, but in professional football the enmity of opposition fans is a badge of honour. The manner in which he diverts criticism of his players towards himself for the sake of the team is exactly what

Jim Collins was referring to when he spoke of professional will and personal humility. It's why you never hear Sir Alex berate a player in public, and why his players, in turn, despite their massive salaries and celebrity status, respond to the manager with such devotion.

Professor Sondhi outlines some further thoughts on professional will:

Professional will comprises a number of factors. Firstly, high performers set inspired standards, which form the focus for the drive that creates success. Prior to 1999, it was thought that no team would ever win the treble of the English Premier League, the English FA Cup and the European Champions League – in fact, no one believed it could be achieved until three minutes before the end of the final game of the 1999 season, between Manchester United and Bayern Munich. United were losing 1-0, having won the two other trophies. The head of UEFA had gone down the lift in Barcelona with the cup, wearing the colours of Bayern Munich. When he arrived at the bottom, he was bewildered – the 'winners' were crying and the 'losers' were celebrating. In those three minutes, United had won the game.

At the club there is the mentality that anything is possible. Simple practices have become part of the history of the club; for example, Sir Alex insists that United should not lose two games in a row. This is ingrained in all the players from the very beginning of their careers with Manchester United. Obviously there have been times when United has lost more than twice in a row (and a few of these occasions involved a blond goalkeeper in the early 1980s), but it certainly doesn't happen often.

One of the main reasons for a lack of success is the fear of failure, which can have a huge impact on an individual's attitude and actions towards achieving a goal. Sir Alex defied all public opinion

in 1995 when he sold Paul Ince, Mark Hughes and Andrei Kanchelskis. Ince was sold because he was apparently starting to think
of himself as bigger than anyone else at the
club, and Sir Alex believed that this would be
detrimental to United. He brought in a group
of youngsters to replace these seasoned
professionals, and was criticised by commentators such as Alan Hansen, who famously
said, 'You'll never win anything with kids.'

One of the main reasons for a lack of success is the fear of failure

That year United won the league and cup double with Scholes,
Beckham, Ryan Giggs, Nicky Butt and the Neville brothers. Sir Alex
has never feared making unpopular decisions.

Another feature of a winning attitude is an intolerance of mediocrity. Leaders accept that any lowering of standards will lead
to a long-term defeat. The types of players
brought in by Sir Alex amplify this attitude,
as illustrated by Roy Keane. South African
player Quinton Fortune says of his former
teammate, 'If you're on Roy Keane's team,
he's not there to lose a game ... If you make
a mistake, or he thinks you're not putting

Another feature of a winning attitude is an intolerance of mediocrity

in the effort, he will have a few days where he's not happy with
you. He wanted you to give the best all the time, and that's just
in training.'

Just like Keane, Sir Alex is known to possess a winning attitude
towards everything he does. He tells the story of how one of his
relatives showed how well he could play the piano one Christmas.
Sir Alex wanted to make sure that he was better than his relative
the next time, so he duly learnt and practised the piano over the
following year with that specific goal in mind. Sir Alex playing the

piano and singing Christmas carols? There's a lot more to him than the figure we see roaring at his team from the dugout.

One other aspect of the winning mentality is the acceptance that you need to look 'out of the window' rather than 'in the mirror'; in other words, focus on moving forward instead of spending too much time reflecting on the past. Since being defeated by Barcelona in the 2011 Champions League final, Sir Alex has spent time studying the new standards set by Barcelona. His attitude was epitomised in an interview conducted after the final. Rather than simply remaining dejected (although he was), Sir Alex said that he was looking forward to the challenge of knocking Barcelona off their perch over the next few years and setting new standards in turn. This is a true indication of a man never willing to stop improving and thus continuing to set new levels of achievement.

In business, there tends to be an acceptance of mediocrity. Sometimes this is due to a lack of focus on goals and a lack of clarity regarding what the leader wants to achieve. In business the quantification of goals and objectives often seems to be far less obvious than in sport. Take your cue from sport, then, and build up a simple but effective framework in which to measure the deliverables you're focused on.

> *The desired outcome needs to be broken down into a 'performance story' that shows how we deliver the end outcome*

This is very dependent on the strategy and vision of the organisation. The desired outcome needs to be broken down into a 'performance story' that shows how we deliver the end outcome. For example, in a football match the end result is dependent on the number of goals scored. The performance story would be, 'We score goals by having more shots at the goal, in particular when they are on target. We can only have shots on goal when we have possession of the ball. Possession is gained by tackling effectively, without committing an offence, and then retaining possession. Once we have possession, we need to move the ball as quickly as possible, without losing possession, into the danger areas on the pitch. The danger areas are those areas where we are most likely to score from.' From the above performance story, we now have the key measures that the Prozone technology uses: number of shots, on target or off target, percentage possession in different areas of the pitch, amount of time the ball is on different parts of the pitch, number of tackles, and so on.

For a sales company, the performance story would run something like this: 'Based on the amount of revenue generated. The revenue is generated by contacting more potential customers and keeping in contact with existing customers. Our existing customers will generate more business for the amount of time spent. To generate more business from our existing customers, we need to ensure that they are happy with our service and product. We can make our customers happy by providing a consistent, high-quality service that exceeds our customers' expectations.' As a result of this story, we will be able to measure revenue, number of new clients, percentage of business from new clients, percentage of business from existing clients, retention of business from existing clients, customer satisfaction, number of complaints, and so on.

To generate more business from our existing customers, we need to ensure that they are happy with our service and product

If you implement the following suggestions, you'll have taken an important step in the right direction.

1. Set the vision and the big goal. Break that goal into smaller components and shorter timescales – in other words, into a source of quick wins, which are essential for building self-belief and self-confidence. The ability to convert a concept into something tangible for the team members is a mark of good leaders.

2. Be clear about the actions needed to achieve these goals, including any training or skills development that is required. In addition, identify the resources needed to deliver the desired outcomes.

Don't be afraid of failure; by learning from failure you ensure that those lessons are built into more successful endeavours in the future.

The following steps will help you to achieve the smaller goals deriving from your overarching objective: Create three goals for the day and strive to achieve them; write down your action plan and identify your resource requirements to achieve these goals; then review your success in achieving them and identify the key learning points from what you've achieved. This is a simple process, but it's one that's rarely implemented. When you discover the impetus it gives your business, you will wonder why you didn't do it earlier.

> *Don't be afraid of failure; by learning from failure you ensure that those lessons are built into more successful endeavours in the future*

TRAINING DAY

Winning leadership is based on developing an appreciation of one-self without seeing others in a better or a worse light. This involves being positive without being arrogant, and thinking of success rather than failure. In addition, winners constantly look to improve and develop, setting new standards and pushing the boundaries of personal and organisational development. Successful individuals also focus on one goal at a time.

To develop these attributes, it is worth reflecting on the questions that follow:

1. What makes you different from everyone else? What are your key strengths?
2. What are the strengths of the people you associate with in the workplace and at home? What can you learn from these people?
3. Do you feel that you are better than some people? List them. Why do you feel that you are better than them? Write down the things you can learn from these people.
4. Do you feel that you are worse than some people? List them. Why do you feel that you are not as good as these people? Make a note of the things they could learn from you.
5. Can you make tough decisions relatively easily? If not, think of an example and try to reframe the decision so that you feel confident in making it.

FULL-TIME TAKEAWAY

- Humility allows you to learn from others (you don't know it all) and to elicit help from others (people don't tend to help those who are arrogant).

- When you are humble you can surround yourself with good people who share your passion for success – don't be afraid to employ the best; not only will you learn from them, but ultimately they will make you look good!
- Professional will encompasses a strong sense of ambition and determination. Tough decisions, sometime ruthless ones, have to be made in order to survive in business, but then focus on being grateful and it will reduce the stress occasioned by making big decisions.
- The ability to reframe situations (discussed in the previous chapter) can aid the decision-making process.

3

Emotional Intelligence

'EI is twice as important as IQ and technical skills. The higher up you go, the more important EI becomes.'

– Daniel Goleman, author

You need only to spend a few minutes outside Liverpool's Anfield ground, Arsenal's Emirates stadium or Chelsea's Stamford Bridge – or indeed any football stadium in England on match day – to hear some colourful opinions on the evils of Sir Alex Ferguson. Arrogant, aggressive, nasty, a bully, lucky to have won what he has ... from fans of United's rivals, there's a lot of vitriol directed at my old boss. And, knowing Sir Alex, he wouldn't have it any other way – he would assume he'd been doing something wrong if Liverpool or Chelsea fans were supporting him.

But plenty of fans from beyond the Church of Old Trafford would also be happy to admit their admiration for the greatest manager of the modern era. They might not always like him, particularly if their team has just lost to United, but the sheer scale of Sir Alex's success can be appreciated by a football community comprised of more than just foul-mouthed thugs and drunken fans. The impression that the malignant core of supporters has sadly given the British game is not reflective of the greater group. Despite what the evidence from the terraces might suggest, I found fans in England, by and large, to be thoughtful, knowledgeable followers of the game. You'd still get a mouthful from the crowd if you slipped up, as I discovered on numerous occasions, but for all their parochial leanings, most of the fans are keen enough followers of football to acknowledge and appreciate a brilliant talent or an outstanding achiever.

Sir Alex fits into both of those categories, although he'd be the last to lay claim to either accolade. His blue-collar background and his own struggles as a player produced a humble man, and this has led to another attribute that plays a crucial role in management of any sort: emotional intelligence (EI).

Two years ago I was at a United training session, enjoying the thrill of watching the team at work in a non-match-day environment. Years as a professional footballer haven't taken away the fan inside me – watching Rooney running off the ball, Ferdinand crunching into a tackle and Giggs at full tilt in defiance of his 37 years made me realise that, while we certainly worked hard when I was at United, the professional game today operates at another pace entirely.

Sir Alex had been kind enough to invite me over to watch the training with him. After a couple of minutes of standing beside him, observing some of the world's best athletes at work, I realised that the manager was as much of a spectator as I was. He issued no directives to players and no commands from the sidelines. Other than the occasional word to the first-team coach, he simply stood with me, looking on as training took place. Sir Alex Ferguson, standing quietly beside a football field? Not an image many people can envision, I imagine.

After 10 minutes or so, I finally asked Sir Alex why he wasn't getting involved. His answer was simple but enlightening. 'I'm observing the players, Gary,' he explained. 'I've got 24 players out there, all great footballers. I need to watch their body language, see who's looking strong and positive and who isn't – and why. That will ensure I can select the best possible team.'

If anything sums up the importance of emotional intelligence, that is it – observation. Having a brilliant left foot or being the best man-marker in the game is only a part of the skills set a player brings to a game; his emotional frame of mind is just as important – on occasion, even more so. A player distracted by relationship issues, homesickness or trouble with the tabloids (a weekly occurrence across the Premiership) will often see his performance affected as a result. There are players who are able to channel that emotion back into football and use 90 minutes on the park to escape from issues away from the game, but, in most cases, major distractions have a negative impact on performance.

There are so many examples that indicate the importance of observation to the success of managers. When interviewed by the former Downing Street spin doctor Alistair Campbell on what made him successful, Sir Alex responded, 'Observation ... spotting everything around you ... analysing what's important, seeing dangers and

There are many examples that indicate the importance of observation to the success of managers

opportunities that others can't see.' Tony Adams says something similar about Arsène Wenger: 'On Friday night before the 1998 FA Cup Final, Arsène sat us down in a team meeting at the hotel in Chelsea we use. "I've been observing everyone since we won the title," he said, "and we have changed. We got here because we were a team, and we looked to our own performance, but lately we have been looking at each other's performances."' It was this realisation, deriving purely from observation – on the part of both Wenger and his players – that allowed Arsenal to go on to clinch the double.

Observation is a crucial component of empathy, which is the word most used to describe emotional intelligence. Empathy consists of four primary actions: observing, evaluating, feeling and responding – all of which are demonstrated in the above examples.

> *Observation is a crucial component of empathy, which is the word most used to describe emotional intelligence*

Of all of Sir Alex's qualities, it is his emotional intelligence that I admire the most: his ability to read his players and to understand what they happen to be going through, and to respond to the situation of the day appropriately. Responsible for managing young guys with a high profile and plenty of money, and the media just waiting for them to slip up, the modern manager's job extends well beyond the realm of the football field, and the successful manager understands this. As Professor Sondhi explains:

Emotional intelligence is the ability to perceive, integrate, understand and regulate emotions in order to facilitate thought and promote personal growth. Many managers and coaches in sport have been noted for their ability to handle people well. According to the Bar-On model of emotional intelligence, developed by Reuven Bar-On, EI is defined as effectively understanding oneself and others, relating well to people, and adapting and coping with one's immediate surroundings in order to be more successful in dealing with environmental demands. Bar-On also suggests that this intelligence is developed over time and is based largely on environment.

Many managers and coaches in sport have been noted for their ability to handle people well

The greatest managers remain in control of their emotions, even though this may not appear to be the case all of the time. Some years ago Sir Alex was seen giving a player a 'telling off' in the dressing room. Some of the player's teammates remarked afterwards that his hair was standing up as if he were under a hairdryer; ever since then a 'telling off' from Sir Alex has been known as 'the hairdryer'. The players know that this is a controlled response to get a message across. Rarely, if ever, does Sir Alex revert to the issue once he's dealt with it. The players hold him in the highest regard, as he is consistent in knowing who needs a stern word and who needs an arm around them, largely from observing his players in their environment, sensitively evaluating their needs and responding appropriately.

My first experience of the infamous hairdryer was in a game against Luton in 1987, my first game for Sir Alex. We conceded a late goal in the first half to allow Luton to level at 1-1 before half-time. I had been injured in the build-up to the World Cup in Mexico the year before and had spent nine months recovering. Although I'd heard about the hairdryer, none of the players would tell me about it in detail, so when we walked into the dressing room, I was watching to see where Sir Alex (just 'Alex' then) would plug in the hairdryer.

Sir Alex walked up to me and asked me what had happened. I replied that I'd thought the cross was mine, but then I'd shouted, 'Away!' It was then up to the fullback, Colin Gibson, to sort out the problem. Sir Alex turned and walked up to Colin, and nose to nose proceeded to tear a strip off my teammate. I witnessed Colin's hair blowing back – and suddenly I realised what the hairdryer was. I made sure I didn't laugh, as I knew that that would be a career-limiting move. As we walked out to resume play, Sir Alex must have seen my puzzlement and perhaps shock at what had just happened. 'Gary,' he said to me, 'there are some players you scream at, and some you talk nicely to. The key is knowing the difference.' That's when I realised

> *'There are some players you scream at, and some you talk nicely to. The key is knowing the difference'*

that this new manager had something different and very special.

Sir Alex is fiercely protective of the team, defending players furiously in the face of the media and drawing the attention to himself. It's a sacrifice he embraces: he's quite happy to be the fall guy if it means that one of his players is relieved of media pressure that could negatively affect performance.

'When I tell them what I think of them, it is in the right place, in the privacy of the dressing room or my office. I will never start slagging players [off] in public,' Sir Alex has explained to *Goal* magazine. 'Once you do that, you have lost the bolt off the dressing-room door. My job is not to criticise my players publicly. When a manager makes a public criticism, he's affecting the emotional stability of a player, and that cannot be the professional thing to do. It's more about loyalty than protection. I'm not interested in what people say about me overprotecting my players. My job is to keep Manchester United and its supporters happy, and make sure those players die for me.'

Think of Sir Alex's handling of the brilliant Wayne Rooney, whom he's coaxed from troublesome hothead to one of the best players in the world, or his treatment of Éric Cantona. There's a rich seam of irony to a Frenchman, temperamental even by Gallic standards, finally finding his spiritual home in England. Cantona's transfer to Manchester United from Leeds United was heralded as a bold move by some, but as an act of lunacy by most. The head-lines decried it as a gamble, and it *was* a risk. But Sir Alex's risks are always carefully calculated – in Cantona, he saw a player who could slot in perfectly at Old Trafford with the right support. And he did, superbly.

But the triumphant Cantona story would not have unfolded at United had it not been for Sir Alex's emotionally intelligent responses to one of the most dramatic incidents the Premier League has seen. Sent off in 1995 against Crystal Palace, Cantona received a torrent of abuse from a leering Palace fan. As only he would have, he responded with a surprisingly agile karate kick that was still being shown on Sky television a week later. It earned the amateur martial artist in the red jersey a nine-month ban from the game.

That could have been the end of Cantona's association with United, the Premiership and possibly even football. He openly admitted that retiring from the game was a serious consideration. Understanding what Cantona's mindset and response were likely to be, Sir Alex took time to visit his suspended player at his home in Paris, offering him support, talking football and reassuring him that he was still very much a part of the set-up at Old Trafford.

Cantona maintains that it was this show of support from his manager that kept him in the game and, by extension, with United.

The result? United won the league with Cantona the following season, despite the team's being well behind Newcastle when he returned from his suspension. United turned it into a double when Cantona, standing in for the injured Steve Bruce as captain, lifted the FA Cup. A year later and Cantona had another league title to his name, a fourth in five years, before he retired as one of the greatest players ever to have worn a United jersey.

Professional football is littered with wasted talent: players with a touch of genius but without the resolve or mental strength to do justice to their footballing ability. Would Éric Cantona have been able to sign off on such a successful career without the guidance of Sir Alex, a man who understood how to get the best out of him? It's unlikely.

> *Professional football is littered with wasted talent: players with a touch of genius but without the resolve or mental strength to do justice to their footballing ability*

'Ferguson always made allowances for Cantona, wisely exempting him from the "hair-dryer treatment",' writes one of Sir Alex's biographers. 'He was the only exception. Once the squad was invited to a reception at Manchester Town Hall, and in advance Ferguson issued strict instructions about dress. Every player turned up immaculate: club blazer, trousers, collar and tie. Except Cantona. He wore a tracksuit and trainers. Any other player would have been sent home. Because it was Cantona, Ferguson pretended not to notice.'

The only response that Ferguson eventually gave, according to the guys in the team at the time, was a shrug of the shoulders and the accepting admission that Cantona was 'a lad'. This was not favouritism; it was simply EI at work.

Other players have attested to this quality in the manager. 'He was good like that, always used to go and see any player who was in hospital for an operation or treatment,' wrote Lee Sharpe in his autobiography. 'He was never one of those managers, all too common in football, who ignore players when they're of no immediate use.'

Ruud van Nistelrooy, the big Dutch striker who missed out on signing for United after a serious injury, offers similar reflection. 'Two days after my injury, Mr Ferguson flew over to Holland to visit me,' Van Nistelrooy told the club's official magazine a year later. 'He was so warm and friendly, it made a big impression on me. From then on he would phone me every four weeks. The way he talked to me was very encouraging. It definitely helped my recovery. The good feelings I had about United gave me strength to fight back.'

A year later, Van Nistelrooy did finally sign for United for £18 million, and Sir Alex's patience and support were rewarded with 150 goals in just 219 appearances for the club.

So how does all of this apply to business? The simplest way of summing it up is to point to the character who is the antithesis of EI and empathy, Basil Fawlty – John Cleese's thick-skinned hotel manager in the cult comedy series *Fawlty Towers*. Aim to be the opposite of Basil and you're headed in the right direction! But while the principles of EI are simple enough to grasp, translating them into effective management style makes for more of a challenge.

The key point of departure is observation. Just as Sir Alex stood observing his team in training to understand what space the players were in, so observing your employees, colleagues, customers and business environment will afford you an understanding of how better to manage your working environment. Knowing when someone needs a kind word or a push in the right direction can dramatically improve his or her effectiveness, and this is an understanding that observation provides. All too often we walk into our communal office space, head straight for our computer, and get cracking with work and phone calls. I think it would be more than worthwhile – and will help you to be more productive in the long run – to spend a few minutes observing those around you and finding out what the burning issues are. It's not just idle chatter, but the building up of emotional intelligence.

It would be more than worthwhile to spend a few minutes observing those around you and finding out what the burning issues are

Here's the prof with more practical thoughts on EI and the power of observation:

Observation is a critical leadership skill, as it improves both the quality of decision-making and the nature of relationships. The things we should take note of when observing people, whether it is customers, staff or competitors, are their perceptions, their opinions, and the facts and emotions they express.

Observation skills can be developed by increasing your curiosity levels. Watch closely what people do in different situations and try to understand why they do these things. Look at people from differing backgrounds and economic situations. Try to appreciate their perspectives, and to understand why they behave in the way that they do. Observation skills can also be enhanced by placing yourself in different environments and experiencing situations with which you are not familiar, especially ones where you have little emotional attachment.

When observing, try to seek clarity. Be conscious of things that are different, and focus on asking questions rather than on expressing opinions. A key factor is to refrain from passing any judgements when making these observations. Clearly, for a leader, the time will come when a judgement or a decision has to be made, but it is necessary first to learn how to seek a deep understanding of an individual through observing and posing questions. One of the most difficult things to do if you hold a position of responsibility is to put aside personal biases and prejudices. This is where the art of questioning is really useful, as it changes your focus to listening rather than telling.

> *One of the most difficult things to do if you hold a position of responsibility is to put aside personal biases and prejudices*

Look back at some United selections after a player has been through a high-profile public issue, and you won't see a uniform response from Sir Alex. Sometimes the player goes straight back into the starting XI, other times it's a spell on the bench or even with the reserves. That's a result of Sir Alex evaluating what he has picked up from observing the player in question and deciding whether off-field distractions will detract from performance, or game time will offer welcome relief. The principle applies equally in business decisions. Will a recently divorced employee benefit from time away, or the diversion of an increased workload? Should bad publicity require a company to adopt a lower profile, or to embark on an aggressive PR campaign? Do you chastise employees for an underperforming project, or provide encouragement and incentive for them – and the business – to bounce back? Working out what's most effective in a particular situation has no universal rule, but depends substantially on EI.

I'll leave it to Bryan Robson, my former teammate and a great player who also later became a manager, to encapsulate the emotional intelligence of Sir Alex Ferguson. 'He does have a softer, human side that the public don't see and probably wouldn't believe. He's not all iron fist,' Robson reveals. 'Just when you expect a rollicking, he'll be very sympathetic and supportive. He cares about his players and all those who work for him.' These words are as applicable to the business world as they are to football, as Professor Sondhi illustrates:

In the business sense, much of the work on EI has been carried out by Daniel Goleman, through his works *Emotional Intelligence* and *Social Intelligence*. Goleman identified the key elements of EI: first, self-awareness, which is attained by knowing your emotions; second, self-management, which allows you to manage your emotions and motivate yourself; third, social awareness, to recognise and understand other people's emotions; and fourth, relationship management, to help manage other people's emotions.

Self-awareness requires people to move outside of their comfort zones to enable them to see how they react to different situations. Owing to the nature of training and exposure to public scrutiny, professional sportspeople have a great opportunity to develop this critical skill. Football managers haven't always been exposed to formal courses providing the skills necessary for the job, but even when they have, much of what they learn is on the job. Forced to stretch their skills into new areas, they make mistakes and (it is to be hoped) learn from them. There are many cases where successful managers

> *Self-awareness requires people to move outside of their comfort zones to enable them to see how they react to different situations*

have not been able to adapt. Very few top-flight clubs in Europe have a manager who has been in charge for a decade or more. Football managers are faced with new players, new opposition and new challenges each season, and Sir Alex is one of the few leaders who has been able to reinvent himself in the constantly changing environment of top-flight professional football.

The basic elements of emotional intelligence – his respect for people and the clarity with which he understands his own emotions – were sown in his background and are integral to his character. Ferguson and Wenger headline a very short list of football managers who have been at the helm for extended periods of time; there are far more leaders in business who have had lengthy spells in charge of big corporations.

> *Self-management is a unique ability to control one's emotions in stressful situations for the benefit of the team*

Self-management is a unique ability to control one's emotions in stressful situations for the benefit of the team. To a degree this is developed from creating an emotional detachment from the situation, which can suggest a paradox, given that the most successful leaders are those who demonstrate passion.

Wayne Rooney offers a great example here of the balance required when it comes to self-management. Few footballers show more commitment over the 90-minute period than Rooney, who frequently tracks back to his own box to harass the opposition, win back possession and kick-start a counter-attack that he'll often finish as well. But in his early years at United, that passion often boiled over into rash challenges, clashes with opponents (particularly older, streetwise defenders who quickly worked out how to push Rooney's buttons) and conversations with referees that gave football some particularly colourful dialogue. While there is still the odd outburst, Rooney's self-management has improved dramatically. The passion and drive have been channelled into his play, and Sir Alex now has a player far less likely to see his 90 minutes cut short by the flourish of a card. Think back to Zinedine Zidane's red card for his headbutt in the 2006 World Cup final. Here was the greatest player in the world at the time, in the biggest game on the soccer calendar, who 'lost it'. Because of that one crazy moment, the Frenchman was sent off and effectively handed the trophy to Italy. This is as vivid an illustration as any of the importance of keeping a handle on your emotions under pressure.

Try to think of three emotional triggers that make you angry in the business environment. Is it when someone criticises you, or when someone doesn't do what they said they would do? Once you have written down these 'hot buttons' and figured out what emotion or previous hurt is causing them, your awareness is increased and you are less likely to react with anger. Self-management is thus crucial in effectively dealing with pressurised situations.

> *Self-management is crucial in effectively dealing with pressurised situations*

Social awareness takes self-management one step further through the understanding of how the people around you feel. What is shaping their emotions, and how is this likely to impact on the performance of the team? This assessment demands complete objectivity, so that the leader's own emotions do not take over. Those who have played under Sir Alex have recalled that he rarely holds grudges against his players. He expresses his concerns in what he feels is the most appropriate form (which may or may not be a high-volume burst of Scottish invective) and then moves on.

Finally, **relationship management** requires close relationships with team members, so that you are able to use the most appropriate form of communication for that particular individual when necessary. In effect, it's the response to the social awareness described above – successful leaders should ask, 'I know how someone is feeling, so how best do I respond?'

> *Successful leaders should ask, 'I know how someone is feeling, so how best do I respond?'*

To reinforce the value of an emotionally intelligent manager, I'll turn to my England boss, Sir Bobby Robson. I remember Sir Bobby with great fondness, not simply because his honest, caring management style elicited a positive response from many of his players, but because of his management of me in 1986 at the World Cup in Mexico.

I hadn't left South Africa for England with any particular hopes of playing international football. The extent of my football dreams (or delusions, as many of my mates cheerfully labelled them) was to play for Manchester United. But when I made good on those dreams with surprising speed and became United's starting keeper, the natural sense of ambition inherent in any professional sportsman saw me recalibrate my footballing horizons. I began to think about playing for England. There were only two problems there: Ray Clemence and Peter Shilton.

England had two exceptional goalkeepers to choose from at the same time. They were both natural shot-stoppers, excellent communicators and outstanding in their positional awareness – which was great for England, but tough if you were an up-and-coming keeper hoping to break into the national team. That, coupled with the injury that brought my career to an end, limited my appearances for England to just two. I did manage to get to a World Cup, however, and though I didn't play in Mexico in 1986, it was still a most instructive period of my personal life.

I had injured my knee in training ahead of the World Cup, which in effect shifted me down the order from number-two goal-keeper (behind Shilton) to number three (behind Chris Woods), Clemence having already retired from international football. In fact, the injury could have knocked me right out of the World Cup, but I went to the pre-tournament training camp in Colorado, and Sir Bobby's loyalty to and belief in me meant that I stayed with the chosen 22 for Mexico. The result was seven weeks of sitting around, with limited training and no game time – in an era without the internet or cable television for distraction. (Mexican television in 1986 wasn't designed with English football teams in mind.) I remember sitting on the roof of our hotel with Chris Woods, counting the number of VW Beetles (they had their own plant in Mexico, so there were loads of them) that drove past and betting on the number we'd see per minute ... not the most exciting way to pass the day.

The mundane activity that the world never sees when a World Cup is under way challenges management to keep players focused and motivated. That challenge is considerably greater when a player is carrying an injury and becomes a peripheral part of the training squad. In 1986, that player was me, and with the pressures of winning a World Cup weighing heavily on Sir Bobby, worrying about keeping his third-choice goalkeeper entertained certainly didn't need to be a priority.

But chief among Sir Bobby's attributes was his caring nature: he took a genuine interest in his players and their welfare. The

World Cup was no exception. He made a point of constantly enquiring about how I was doing and making me feel like a part of the squad. And it was more than a token gesture to keep me feeling upbeat: Sir Bobby made sure I knew that if something happened to Shilton and Woods took the keeper's jersey, I'd be ready to have my knee drained, receive a cortisone injection and take my place on the bench. That Sir Bobby valued my experience enough to trust me with the back-up position – and trust my assurances that I was ready if needed – not only kept my spirits high, but would also, I'm certain, have carried me through my injury had I been needed as an emergency replacement.

Chief among Sir Bobby's attributes was his caring nature: he took a genuine interest in his players and their welfare

In the end I wasn't required, and England's tournament ended in a quarter-final remembered for the genius and opportunism of Diego Maradona, who took Argentina to their second World Cup triumph.

John Barnes, an England teammate of mine in 1986, relates a similar story about how Sir Bobby always got you wanting to play for him. Before a big international match, Barnsie was called in to see the manager, who just couldn't bring himself to tell Barnes that he wasn't the right man for the job. Sir Bobby started off by saying that he needed younger legs up front. Then he said that Peter Beardsley's legs were too short and he couldn't cover the required ground, that Gary Lineker had a stomach bug ... and then he blurted out: 'John, you're just not playing that well.' Barnsie says that he didn't feel angry, but rather supportive of his manager, because he had tried so hard not to upset or deflate him.

Here is some slightly more academic support for the value of EI from Professor Sondhi.

A variety of emotional responses may be used to maximise the effect of messages being conveyed to team players. Top leaders have an ability to utilise the full spectrum of emotional responses. These include sadness, disgust, anger, fear, happiness and love. In the past, leaders may have viewed these softer responses as a sign of weakness. Even in the military, where many of the tougher responses have traditionally been used, the value of EI is increasingly appreciated. Army patrols might not be starting with a group hug for the platoon each day, but there's been a definite shift in leadership style from the one-dimensional, screaming sergeant-major of old. Only by knowing the individual and his or her needs and moods will the leader be able to gauge the most appropriate response. Clearly, a more outward-looking leader is going to be more effective in this regard than a more inward-looking one.

> *Only by knowing the individual and his or her needs and moods will the leader be able to gauge the most appropriate response*

The key emotional competencies that need to be developed for the emotionally intelligent leader are influence, team leadership, organisational awareness, self-confidence, drive and empathy. It is easy to list them, but these competencies are not quite so easy to master. So, where to begin? Understanding and improving the connection between emotions and actions is the first step towards business and personal success.

Firstly, it is important to understand your own level of EI and how you react to stressful situations. This can be achieved by consciously noting what your feelings are in a variety of situations involving a range of people, as described earlier. Observe how you react and learn to label your feelings rather than labelling people or situations: what somebody does in a work situation isn't necessarily reflective of the person he or she is.

Allow me to interject quickly in support of this point. All goalkeepers think they have a divine right to scream abuse at defenders who aren't in position, miss tackles or lose the player being marked. But for all the angry interaction you might see on the field, it's almost always left there. Mistakes on the field are not reflective of a player's nature or character; as footballers, we all know and understand that. The same is true of a working environment: failure to complete a project or deliver on a task often leads to criticism of a personal nature rather than criticism of the failures themselves. Here is further guidance in that vein from Professor Sondhi:

Take responsibility for what you feel. Express statements that put you in control of your emotions. Sir Alex frequently makes declarations that establish his control of a situation and eliminate the notion that he is reacting rashly. You might not always agree with his methods – such as his extended refusal to conduct interviews with anyone from the BBC after taking umbrage at comments made in a television programme about his son – but this reflects a manager creating his own terms of engagement. Top managers use the prism of the media to project their views, manage perceptions and engineer the image of their teams – all of which reflects EI on a grand scale.

There is also the issue of stress. Examining how you react to stressful situations is a fundamental step on the path towards greater emotional awareness. What are your emotional triggers, and how do you respond to them? Do you blame others, or do you get upset when something does not happen the way you want it to? Next time you're watching a game on television, wait for the interview with the losing man-ager and listen out for the list of penalties that weren't given, off-sides that weren't awarded and red cards that should have been dished out to the opposition. It makes for entertaining viewing,

Examining how you react to stressful situations is a fundamental step on the path towards greater emotional awareness

but it's a standard response to defeat: shifting the blame to suggest that factors beyond your control were responsible for the loss. In public, it's the referee, the linesmen and the luck of the opposition at fault; behind the dressing-room doors, however, it's usually a very different story. While television allows the manager to explain to the world that defeat is not the fault of the team or manager, in a private setting the manager tends to make it extremely clear who he believes to be at fault.

Crucial here is the manager's understanding, and emotional awareness, of the defeat his team has suffered. Publicly, he wants the world to side with his team, make the case for victimhood, point out the refereeing inconsistencies that brought down his team. In the far more intimate team environment, however, away from the media soap opera, he needs to decide whether the team needs to be uplifted and consoled, or given a dressing down for poor performance. It illustrates the multifaceted nature of the emotional intelligence that a manager is required to possess and exercise – but also provides a pointer to the business leader.

Facing the media as a CEO after your stock price has fallen might necessitate one message; speaking to your staff in an attempt to reverse that trend may well require another message entirely. Whether it's three points lost at home or 3 per cent off the share price, you're dealing with a particularly stressful situation. It is useful to spend time identifying the best stress-busting techniques for you: what calms you down, relaxes you, allows you to breathe more easily when pressure builds up? The first stage of understanding and improving your emotional intelligence is about building self-awareness.

Managing your stress levels, and learning to give yourself time to provide emotionally intelligent responses, is crucial to becoming someone who can perform under pressure. Emails of an emotional nature, for instance – a response to criticism, say, or unhappiness with a colleague – should be left in your outbox for an hour or overnight before you send them. Reread them before letting them go; there's a good chance that a cooler head will allow for more balanced correspondence, and thus more effective dialogue.

Managing your stress levels, and learning to give yourself time to provide emotionally intelligent responses, is crucial to becoming someone who can perform under pressure

A quick word to back up Professor Sondhi here: early on in my time in England, well before CDs, iPods or any of the other technology that mysteriously appears on my credit card statement every time my kids take me shopping, we had cassette tapes. As I mentioned earlier, I made myself a tape of messages that affirmed how lucky I was to be at Manchester United, what an incredible opportunity I had and why I needed to make the most of it. Listening to that tape on the way to training or a game, and again on the way back, was a simple thing to do, but the results were appreciable: I'd get to training a calmer, more positive person, ready to take on the world with a smile on my face and a skip in my step.

Whatever your tape is, metaphorically speaking, you need to find it. That's part of understanding your own EI. As the professor makes clear below, however, it is necessary to extend that understanding beyond yourself and to take steps to welcome the changes you need to make, all the while being grateful for the opportunity to do so.

You need to demonstrate an understanding and acceptance of other people's feelings by building up empathy towards them. It's all well and good to understand yourself, but that is only a point of departure for understanding the people with whom you work and communicate. Validating other people's emotions by rephrasing and restating their feelings is a simple but

> *You need to demonstrate an understanding and acceptance of other people's feelings by building up empathy towards them*

effective method to use to demonstrate an understanding of how they feel or what they are saying. Use these feelings to show respect for others. Listen to how they feel about your position, and learn to take their feelings into consideration – while someone's opinion or contribution might not change a decision or an approach, knowing that they have been heard and considered makes people feel included in the process at hand, and builds up confidence and goodwill as a result. Focusing on listening with empathy rather than judgement, as discussed earlier, means that your effectiveness as a leader will improve overnight. It honestly is that simple.

In an extension of this application of empathy, it is necessary to learn how to resolve conflicts in ways that build trust. This means ensuring that discussions are based on facts rather than on past issues or existing prejudices. Try to avoid carrying baggage with you into arguments, as this can cloud the possibility of a beneficial solution. You need to be clear about what is actually being discussed or debated. Sometimes you have to accept that some arguments will not be resolved, so be prepared to walk away from these.

Focusing on listening with empathy rather than judgement means that your effectiveness as a leader will improve overnight

Anyone who's seen a goalkeeper in full cry after he feels his defenders have let him down – and I certainly climbed into teammates on occasion – might feel that we have a lot to learn about EI. In the heat of those moments, the defenders in question may well have agreed, but in truth we had EI worked out pretty well, even if we didn't realise it at the time. The discussions after the match would focus on the game's shortcomings and we'd sort them out, knowing how important it was for the team to go forward. You get a feel for your teammates in the heat of a match, and that extends to the dressing room afterwards. You don't always get it right, but you generally know when a player needs a pat on the back, a laugh or just some quiet time on his own. Sir Alex has exhibited a more polished understanding of this, as discussed, but I'll leave you with one final example of the value of EI from a leader in an entirely different sport.

The night before rugby's World Cup final in 2007, South Africa's coach, Jake White, delivered a handwritten letter to every single member of the team he had taken to France, and who had in turn seen the Springboks through to the championship match against England. He could have been spending time with his family or meeting the media to gain from his success, but instead he chose to handwrite 15 letters. In those letters, White highlighted the contributions the player in question had made in the tournament, emphasised how proud he was of every one of them, and stressed the pride that the players had brought to their families, their friends and a country waiting in hopeful expectation. White also mentioned the school each player had been to, as well as the names of the school coaches and the players' parents.

The following day, South Africa saw off England in Paris in a victory grounded in self-belief. No scientific measurement can say exactly how important the letters White wrote to his players were. But there's a World Cup trophy that confirms the inspired leadership that Jake White brought to his job. On the pressure-cooker eve of the biggest game of his life, simply putting pen to paper might just have been the final push South Africa needed to win a World Cup. Emotional intelligence really is that important.

Developing emotional intelligence is a lengthy process that involves much internal assessment

TRAINING DAY

Developing emotional intelligence is a lengthy process that involves much internal assessment. As with other elements of leadership, the key is to understand ourselves and appreciate others in order to optimise the effectiveness of the group. To comprehend our emotions and those of others fully, we need to be able to reflect on a variety of situations that take us outside of our comfort zones. It is necessary to recognise how we respond under pressure, as this provides us with a truer reflection of our responses. It is very easy to assume that, in the moment, we shall behave in the appropriate manner, but the acid test is producing the appropriate behaviour under stress. The following questions will help in this quest. Remember to write down your responses to these questions in a logbook, in the form of an essay.

1. **What emotions do you display?**

   In your typical day, how much time do you spend expressing sadness, anger, happiness, disgust, fear and love? Is this acceptable to you? Go through each of the emotions listed and identify the situations that led to experiencing these emotions, and for how much time you found yourself in this state. Reflect on your personal level of satisfaction with the amount of time spent in each of these states.

2. **How do you respond to different people in different situations?**

   Reflect on your interactions with people in a range of environments, including the workplace, and list the emotions that manifested themselves with those people. What was the reason for those emotions? What level of pressure or stress did you feel while interacting with those people? Why did you experience these pressures? This set of reflections is designed to assess how you respond to different people and in a variety of states of stress.

3. **How do people respond to you?**

   Reflect on your interactions with a number of different people and list the emotions (as in Question 1 above) that you perceive them to have felt while interacting with you.

Why do you think that they experienced these emotions? What level of pressure or stress do you believe they felt in interacting with you during these situations? Why do you think they felt these pressures?

4. **What kind of person would you like to be?**
   What emotions would you like to have felt in the interactions and situations listed above? What is the extent of the gap between your actual and your desired levels of emotion?

FULL-TIME TAKEAWAY

- Emotional intelligence is about behaving in a way that satisfies you and delivers the desired outcome. To do that you need to focus on your inner ability to cope with pressure and derive satisfaction from your work, and then to harness empathy (starting with observation) to achieve your desired objectives.
- Self-awareness involves understanding yourself.
- Self-management entails managing your emotional triggers so that your responses are emotionally intelligent.
- Social awareness involves observing others, refraining from judgement, asking questions and remaining objective.
- Relationship management means making the time and the effort with others in order to facilitate appropriate responses.

4

Adaptability

'When you stop learning, you stop
developing and growing, you stop
becoming agile, and that's the END!'
– A.G. Lafley, CEO of Procter & Gamble

The City Ground, Nottingham, 1984.

For the second week running we had been 2-0 up, and for the
second week running we'd lost 3-2, this time after Dutch centre
back Johnny Metgod, who'd signed for Nottingham Forest from
Real Madrid that season (not a move I can envisage any of the
Galácticos making today), scored a last-minute free kick. The atmosphere in the changing room afterwards wasn't terribly good. I was
in a foul mood; so too, it turned out, was Gordon McQueen, our
six-foot-five defender who'd grown up in a tough neighbourhood
in Glasgow. I made some comments about his defending, and he
responded with some choice opinions on my goalkeeping. The

next thing I knew, he'd all but knocked me out with one hell of a punch. Luckily for him, one of my teammates held me back; luckily for me, the rest of the squad held Gordon back.

This incident and the events that followed sound like the opening scenes of a bad martial arts movie, something that Chuck Norris or Steven Seagal would lay claim to. Realising that I needed to be a stronger, harder man to deal with that sort of situation, I went off to Manchester's Chinatown and found my way to Steve Powell, a martial arts expert. I spent the next four years training with him, and it brought complete physical and attitudinal trans-formation.

A year and a half into my new training regime, when I mistimed a clearing kick and broke the ribs of Aston Villa's Colin Gibson (who would later play for United), my teammates were convinced that I'd used my new talents to do it on purpose. I never denied it ... and never had another problem in the dressing room.

The point to be made here (other than the fact that Éric Cantona is not the only Manchester United alumnus with a penchant for martial arts) is that I needed to make a change in order to flourish in my new environment. I didn't drink much, I had a degree in a team of guys who largely hadn't been to university or even finished school, I was from a distant and very different part of the world, and, in retrospect, I'd let the differences isolate me from my teammates. My clash with McQueen simply brought it all to a head. It made me realise that I wanted to be able to look after myself if necessary (although taking on angry six-foot-five Glaswegians is something I've thankfully avoided since). For the first time I understood that, if I was going to get the best out of my football career in England, I had to adapt to my environment.

And so the martial arts training served two purposes: it tough-ened me up physically, giving me a stronger physique and greater confidence in my physical ability and power; and it created a tough image that gained me the respect of my peers. For the first time I began to truly appreciate the importance of adaptability.

Adaptability is something that's been absolutely crucial to Sir Alex's enduring success and longevity

Adaptability is something that's been absolutely crucial to Sir Alex's enduring success and longevity. Many coaches have competed with United's manager in the Premiership and in Europe, beating him to trophies or outpacing him in the drawn-out sprint that is the league season. But none have come close to matching him over the long run: success has been fleeting in comparison.

Look back over the managers Sir Alex has locked horns with in the past two decades, and you have some of the continent's finest: Kenny Dalglish, Fabio Capello, Arsène Wenger, Marcello Lippi, José Mourinho and Pep Guardiola – all extremely good managers, certainly, but all who have either had short runs with a particular club, such as Mourinho, or been unable to sustain their success, like Wenger. During all this time, Sir Alex has consistently produced strong, competitive and successful teams. One of his former players at Aberdeen, Billy Stark, said: 'I think the biggest compliment you can

I think the biggest compliment you can pay Alex Ferguson is that for all the changes that have taken place in football, he has always adapted

pay Alex Ferguson is that for all the changes that have taken place in football, he has always adapted.'

Sir Alex himself understands the need to adapt, even when he doesn't like some of the changes to the football world. During a talk to students in Dublin, he mused, 'When somebody scored, everyone used to celebrate together. Today they run across to the crowd ... I don't know whether it's self-adulation or what. Tattoos, earrings – it's not my world – but I've had to adjust to it!'

My challenge as a young goalkeeper was to understand the new culture surrounding me. A manager's challenge is to turn the prospect of an ageing squad into an opportunity for growth by bringing in new, exciting talent, which will keep the squad invigorated and primed for competition. In fact, if you look at how Sir Alex has changed, and consider that very few of his contemporaries have managed to follow him, it makes you realise how difficult it really is.

Initially he was the tough manager, demanding success on the pitch and giving players the hairdryer treatment if they didn't comply. He knew that in the heat of the 90-minute battle he had to inspire and even scare players into performing – and in those days you couldn't just get up and leave the club, so you had to take the criticism and respond.

Then, with the 1995 Bosman ruling, he had to change tack because players could get upset with that sort of treatment and legally demand a move. He realised that the best way to create fear and produce success on the pitch was by hiring someone like himself, but someone who was also a player and could get away with shouting at the players. Cue Roy Keane – the supreme warrior in the mould of the manager.

By the early 2000s, even more adaption was necessary. A foreign contingent started pouring into the Premier League to reap the income from the new, substantial television deals now on offer. Juan Sebastián Verón, Cristiano Ronaldo, Diego Forlán and José Kléberson arrived on the scene, all with a different approach to football from that of the dogged northern Europeans. Communication between these players and Sir Alex or Roy Keane was strained, so another adaption was necessary, this time in the form of Carlos Queiroz, a talented coach who could speak six languages. After that, there was no room for any foreign player to say that he didn't understand the instructions! The latest adaption, as assistant coach Mike Phelan, an important part of an excellent support team, explained to me, is that Sir Alex now delegates a much larger chunk of his duties in order to reserve his energy for the big decisions.

As the epigraph to this chapter suggests, if you are not improving, learning or staying in touch with the changing times, you will become less agile and less able to function in the world. Your competitors will move in and grab your opportunities, and you could ultimately end up having to close down your business.

If you are not improving, learning or staying in touch with the changing times, you will become less agile and less able to function in the world

So how do we adapt? First, it is necessary to put the ego aside, admit that there are many things you don't know and realise that by learning from others, you can improve yourself and continue to succeed. This might sound like a simple step, but many good business people – and football managers – have stuck with the 'it's worked for me till now, so why should I change it?' speech. As a result, many of these leaders disappear with the changing times.

Assuming that you agree there's a need to keep up with the latest thinking, there are certain major areas that require focus. It's imperative to learn more about yourself, then your colleagues (or teammates) and, finally, your environment.

I certainly learnt more about myself in that dressing room at

Nottingham Forest. I realised the importance of making changes that would help me settle into the footballers' culture, which would result in leading me to achieving greater success. My teammates also had to learn certain things about me in order to get more from me. For a perfect example, let's fast-forward to the final years of my footballing career back in South Africa.

I played in front of the noisiest, most devoted and at times most aggressive fans during my career in England, but for sheer colour and spectacle in the stands, nothing touches Kaizer Chiefs, the club I represented all too briefly after I returned to South Africa from Manchester in the late 1980s. The country's most popular club, the black and gold dazzled from the stands when I made my debut under a weight of expectation even Old Trafford had never placed on me. South African football is full of superstition, and there was a strong belief among our fans that, having played for Manchester United, I would be unbeatable in goal. There were numerous discussions on the radio and television about my superhuman powers, but all in the local languages that I didn't understand, so I was oblivious to the cult status that was building. Imagine the silence, then, when on my debut – against our bitter rival, Orlando Pirates – they scored with their first attack!

In retrospect, it was no bad thing, as it ended any suggestion of my superhuman powers in goal. Entertaining as the rumours of my goalkeeping prowess were, they did me no favours. We went on to draw that game, but that cold dose of reality forced Chiefs fans and players to recalibrate their expectations. The year 1988 ended up being a mixed one for Chiefs, but we went on to win just about everything in 1989, and the Manchester United export clawed back a little respect from the fans after that early setback.

But, just as I'd adapted to another new and different environment, so the supporters and players had adapted their thinking. I received incredible support from them when I first joined Kaizer Chiefs (and still do), but they realised after my debut for the club that, having played for Manchester United, impressive as that might have sounded, didn't make me invincible. There had been adaptation all round – from me, my teammates and the fans, and a year later everyone was smiling.

Adaptability in football offers a particularly close parallel with understanding talent in business

Learning about and keeping up with the changes in your environment is the third focus area for adaptability. Adaptability in football offers a particularly close parallel with understanding talent in business, especially in a world where the pace of technological change can render products obsolete in mere months. Not a week goes by when my kids don't pester me for the latest offering from Apple, the company that has set the benchmark for speed of product development. (Had I written this during my football career, it would have been pounded out on a typewriter; I'm not sure my kids would know what a typewriter is.)

Golf is another arena in which product development and enhancement work at a furious pace (although I'm not sure how much impact new technology actually has in golf ... I still spend most rounds in thick rough, my clubs and I at odds on the approach to the game).

Across any field of endeavour, there's always someone looking to improve, innovate, enhance, invent

Across any field of endeavour, there's always someone looking to improve, innovate, enhance, invent. Which means that you and

115

your business need to be doing exactly the same to ensure that you stay competitive. To do so, you need to focus on and monitor the changes happening in your environment.

The football comparison is the transfer market. In an ideal world, clubs would develop star talent from within and mirror the passage of Ferguson's golden generation of Beckham and Co. into first-team football. The game is now obsessed with instant gratification, however. Fans have always wanted a winning team, but with owners and shareholders now calling the shots, the onus is on managers to go out and buy players to provide the quick fix that will transform a team into league contenders overnight and guarantee competition in Europe.

Simply buying a superstar doesn't always work, however, as Chelsea fans will ruefully acknowledge (United fans too – Juan Sebastián Verón springs to mind). Managers need to find a player who addresses the squad's weaknesses, fits in with the current style of play and will ultimately create a stronger team. This the manager has to do without throwing the club's transfer budget out of the window. 'Evolve immediately' is an apt Nike slogan. In football, as in business, it's not always such an easy task.

While the transfer market in the business world isn't as clear-cut an entity, the movement of employees from firm to firm is well established. Star talent is followed by corporate headhunters who have been given a missive by companies to bring in a top account manager or a proven analyst. It's an environment every bit as cut-throat as football: a senior manager at HSBC moving to Goldman Sachs, say, or a director ditching BMW for Audi, is making no less a shift of allegiance than if I'd left Old Trafford for Anfield. By way of a more recent example, it is a shift as serious as Carlos Tévez's crossing the divide to the blue half of Manchester. But those moves do happen, and for exactly the same reason that they happen in football: a company, like a team, needs to keep improving and adapting. Bringing in new employees with new or stronger skills is crucial to that process. The leader needs to start by better understanding him- or herself, the team dynamics, and, finally, the environment within which he or she operates.

A company, like a team, needs to keep improving and adapting

Social media is a simple example. As Facebook, Twitter and other social networking sites have taken off, large companies have had to adopt a social media strategy to address a market that now interacts extensively on platforms that simply didn't exist a decade ago. They've had to allocate budget accordingly, and either train staff to manage these new channels of communication or bring in outside help. Exactly the same process was at play when Sir Alex brought in Van Nistelrooy to address the club's shortfalls in Europe. Whatever the environment, adaptation is vital to success.

Professor Sondhi suggests below that structure in an organisation is crucial, but an inability to move outside the parameters of that structure or adapt when a situation renders the structure inappropriate can become fatal weaknesses in an organisation:

A clear and well-defined structure in an organisation is imperative

Structure eliminates uncertainty for staff, provides consistency in delivery and allocates appropriate responsibility to relevant people. A clear and well-defined structure in an organisation is imperative. But in sport, an over-structured team can prove to be detrimental. To understand the disadvantage of over-structuring in sports teams, imagine the right back in a football match standing on the six-yard line in the opposition area, refusing to shoot the ball into an empty net because shooting doesn't fall under his defined role. An extreme example, perhaps, but this frequently happens in business, when employees fail to carry out certain functions despite being in an advantageous position, or possessing the knowledge and skills, to do so. Clearly, some degree of structure is required to ensure that resources are used most effectively, but flexibility is a key component of a succesful team.

> *Flexible teams with loosely defined structures are critical in ensuring adaptability in sport*

Flexible teams with loosely defined structures are critical in ensuring adaptability in sport. Such teams need to comprise people with core skills, but also with extended abilities that may be relevant at certain times. In football, the core skills tend to be passing, shooting, dribbling, control and heading the ball – the basics. All players need to possess a certain level of ability in each of these areas to enable them to participate in the whole game, but they also need extended skills such as leadership, drive and confidence, and the capacity to use those skills at various stages of the game.

Even goalkeepers, as Gary will confirm, require more skills than ever before: headers to clear back passes, tackles outside the box when the offside trap has been sprung, and making a run into the opposition box in the 93rd minute in desperate search of an equaliser. There are exceptions in some sports, such as the designated kicker in American football, but by and large having only one string to your sporting bow counts against you in this fiercely competitive era of sporting all-rounders.

In the football world more recently, extended skills have included being able to play in various positions during the course of a match.

The mid-1970s Dutch team of Johan Cruyff was built around the notion of 'Total Football', which involved team members moving around the pitch quite freely. A similar approach has been adopted by Sir Alex at Manchester United. When new players are introduced, particularly young players, they are played in a variety of positions before a dominant position is found for them. In games, this allows for a range of team formations to take place.

Interestingly, a number of other managers, among them Guardiola, Mourinho and Wenger, have adopted similar approaches. Mourinho has frequently used the first half of matches as his research-laboratory opportunity. It's not a strategy you want to implement in important matches, so it often shows itself in pre-season friendlies, reserve games or lesser cup competitions. When it comes to key games, players then have a degree of familiarity with playing multiple roles. They are more flexible members of the team and thus more valuable.

When this thinking is extended to business, several core skills become identifiable, including creative thinking, problem solving, writing and communication. The airline industry provides an excellent example of the pros and cons of adaptability in the business world. This industry was always bound by formal structures, and airline staff had different roles with clear boundaries and specific job descriptions, largely due to the serious consequences of things going wrong. With workers limited to very particular spheres of operation, staff numbers were high, as were costs, and procedures such as aircraft turnarounds were long, drawn-out affairs.

Then American company Southwest Airlines came along and challenged the existing boundaries that afforded so narrow an operational space for employees. Reducing costs and reducing turnaround times were high on Southwest's list of objectives, and the impact was impressive. The airline reduced its Boeing 737 turnaround time from two hours to 20 minutes, for example. This worked out to be the equivalent of having an extra aircraft flying for a full year, thus increasing the efficiency and profitability of the company.

A key feature of football teams such as Manchester United, Arsenal, Chelsea, Barcelona and Real Madrid is the amount of possession they have of the ball. In some games, they will hold the ball for nearly 70 per cent of the time. This is vital to adaptability, as it's very difficult to change your game if you do not have the ball. In business terms, the company needs to be in control of the primary resources to ensure adaptability: the old adage of not being able to play without the ball holds particularly true as a business metaphor.

The old adage of not being able to play without the ball holds particularly true as a business metaphor

The key to being adaptable is to focus on your core competencies, and from there to build a culture that's comfortable with change. In addition, it's important to set positive visions that stretch and engage employees so that the company is constantly striving for improvement in the most appropriate ways. Adaptability also means that the organisation or team needs to have the capacity to handle the risk associated with change. You won't always get it right, but you will be building a culture that is comfortable experimenting with different approaches and can handle risk at different levels before fully committing to a certain direction.

Sir Alex would be the first to concede that a working-class Scottish background isn't the ideal platform from which to understand or work with a flamboyant Brazilian midfielder, say, or a temperamental Ivorian striker. But, as mentioned earlier when discussing the shrewd introduction of Carlos Queiroz to help harness Latin footballing talent at Old Trafford, Sir Alex does have a keen awareness both of the need to adapt and of his own limitations in doing so. That he understands the universal language of football like few others is advantageous here, certainly, but the leagues of Europe are full of intelligent students of the game with astute perceptions of the mechanics involved. None of them, however, can match Sir Alex's ability to adapt to the quicksilver nature of a game in constant flux – or, just as importantly, illustrate that blend of courage and instinct in knowing when to make crucial decisions.

For an even better example of how adapting to new situations can make them work, Professor Sondhi describes Sir Alex's success with Éric Cantona.

The adaptable leader possesses many characteristics, one of which is being comfortable dealing with unconventional team players. In the football arena, Éric Cantona was a classic example of a player who could not find a home until Sir Alex signed him, as discussed briefly in Chapter 3. Cantona played the game very differently from the way that conventional coaches understood it. There was an emotional element to his game that made him a footballing genius, but in the wrong hands this same element could turn him into a liability.

Sir Alex discovered that the best way to embrace a genius such as Cantona was to build the team around him. The coach used other players to make up for some of Cantona's weaknesses – in defending, for example – but the player's sense of creativity and adventure ensured that he was able to deliver the unusual and the unexpected at any time.

Sir Matt Busby had George Best, who also had the ability and confidence to turn the tables. Individuals like Cantona and Best are essential in teams that believe anything is possible and thus embrace adaptability. Paul Gascoigne, Gianfranco Zola, Matt Le Tissier and Franck Ribéry are more recent examples of the same type of player.

> *Individuals like Cantona and Best are essential in teams that believe anything is possible and thus embrace adaptability*

I've often wondered what it must have been like to play with Best or Cantona, footballers who operated at a level that honestly did make the game look too simple. Cantona in particular is a fascinating figure, a curious hybrid of sporting genius, self-styled philosopher, Gallic cult figure and unpredictable talent. But I don't remember any of his United teammates making critical comments about him, other than the occasional remark about his quirky behaviour. That suggests an environment in which his particular brand of genius was allowed to flourish without judgement or resentment – which goes back once again to a manager working alchemy in the transfer market.

I find it fascinating to compare the differences between managers in their attitudes to adaptability. Arsène Wenger has been a staunch representative of stability and consistency over his long reign at Arsenal. However, he is adamant that he will not compromise his style in order to win. Consequently, at the time of writing, Arsenal has not won a trophy for seven years.

Wenger's focus is admirable in an industry in which success is measured in trophies won, and few managers have balanced the club's books as judiciously as Wenger, but the board at Arsenal have demonstrated a degree of patience with their manager that's increasingly rare in professional football. Wenger surely needs to learn and adopt a new approach. Perhaps a few boring 1-0 wins that made the Tony Adams era so famous might not go amiss. Ultimately, though, the manager needs to adapt his style to win trophies and, at the same time, maintain the standard and style of football about which he is so uncompromising.

Sir Alex has had to adapt his style to cope with footballers from different cultures, as Gary has mentioned already. In his early years at United, Sir Alex was able to get the best out of Scandinavian footballers, but he struggled with footballers from Latin backgrounds, Juan Sebastián Verón being the classic example. As Gary suggested, bringing in Carlos Queiroz was as shrewd a signing as Sir Alex has ever made. The coach has subsequently made great strides in the way he gets the best out of those players for whom Manchester is a far cry from the sunshine and samba of their home footballing environments, and he continues to employ excellent foreign coaches, who bring an extra dimension to training sessions.

Contrast that with the best of the new generation of managers: José Mourinho. Mourinho has yet to face a situation that requires serious adaptability, as he hasn't stayed long enough at a single club to do so. His approach is highly dynamic, which has brought him success at a variety of clubs, but he has always moved on rather than seeking to create a legacy through long-term success. This has been the case at Porto, Chelsea, Inter Milan and, possibly, at Real Madrid, where he is stationed at the time of writing. Each of these clubs has seen a dramatic fall in success once Mourinho has left.

Having said that, Chelsea did win the European Champions League in 2012, but the extent to which this success was due to long-term management is debatable. Mourinho also tends to leave on the back of some level of conflict, which doesn't make for a smooth transition of managerial power. The question to be asked here is whether Mourinho is simply a great short-term manager who makes the necessary changes to bring instant success, or whether he can step up to being a great leader, which most people define as someone who can build sustainable success, even after he or she has moved on.

Pep Guardiola hasn't occupied his role for long enough for an accurate assessment of his adaptability to be made, but in the 2011/12 season, Barcelona failed to win anything. This was followed by Guardiola's resignation for a sabbatical. There was the suggestion that this was pre-planned, and perhaps it was (the pressure of coaching Barcelona is enormous), but it was also the first time in the young manager's career that he faced a performance-related issue that might have required some adaptability on his part.

It's not just Professor Sondhi who has picked up on Sir Alex's adaptability: former United stalwart Brian McClair sums up this aspect of his old manager perfectly. 'When it comes to making decisions, he just makes them, whether it's picking a team or buying a player,' writes McClair in his autobiography. 'He makes up his mind, and that's it. He doesn't agonise or prevaricate. If the decision he makes is wrong, he holds his hand up and says he's made a mistake. Tactically there could be times when you fault him, but his successes have proved him right in the long term.' This ability to make decisions confident in the knowledge that there is no failure, only learning, is crucial in assessing adaptability.

Ryan Giggs makes a similar point with regard to United's acquisition of Ruud van Nistelrooy. 'As things turned out, the gaffer's faith in Ruud was repaid in full,' Giggs says. 'Sir Alex had decided to change the way we played in Europe, he felt we'd become too predictable, and Ruud was brought in with that in mind.'

As illustrated earlier, Van Nistelrooy's phenomenal strike rate, particularly in Europe, where he remains the club's all-time highest scorer, more than justified Sir Alex's investment in him. Throughout Sir Alex's career at Old Trafford there are examples of players brought in to build, strengthen and diversify the squad. Peter Schmeichel, Éric Cantona, Ole Gunnar Solskjær, Andrei Kanchelskis, Jaap Stam, Wayne Rooney, Cristiano Ronaldo – the list of Ferguson signings who have caught the imagination and brought about change at Old Trafford is lengthy. There have been players who haven't quite set the club alight, certainly, but one Cantona or Ronaldo comfortably outweighs the combined disappointment of the Djemba-Djembas, Klébersons and Veróns.

Adaptability isn't always about external acquisition, though; appreciating assets closer to home can be equally valuable. The generation of talent that Sir Alex nurtured and transformed into an all-conquering team remains the benchmark for European football development: Paul Scholes, David Beckham, Nicky Butt, Ryan Giggs and the brothers Neville are all part of the same youth side that was scorned when elevated to first-team football, but was soon admired and then feared by the rest of Europe. Granted, the talent must be there in the first place, but few managers would have had the courage and foresight to promote such a large group so early in their careers. Sir Alex appreciated the potential of these players, but also the value in bringing the group through the ranks together, affording them a level of comfort and security that brought them to the fore in so short a time period.

And this has been a crucial aspect of Sir Alex's continual reinvention of Manchester United: driving forward positive sentiment and creating an environment in which change lifts and strengthens a squad. 'What I wanted to show,' Ferguson is reported as saying in his biography, 'was a willingness to promote anyone who did well in the reserves. The worst thing for an older player is to lose his place to a younger man. It's the best competition you can ever get in a football club.'

Sir Alex has shown faith in his players throughout his tenure, but he's also resisted the temptation to hang on to players out of sentiment, as he showed with Roy Keane, whom he sold as soon as Keane's form began to wane. An awareness of the value of a competitive team environment, where performance and commitment are rewarded, has been a sound and enduring principle of life at Old Trafford under Sir Alex. Professor Sondhi recalls a watershed moment at United, driving home this point and emphasising the need to retain the competitive edge:

> *Sir Alex has shown faith in his players throughout his tenure, but he's also resisted the temptation to hang on to players out of sentiment*

An interesting feature of leaders who demonstrate adaptability is the tendency to try the unthinkable. In the 1995/96 season, as mentioned already, Sir Alex sold three key players – Mark Hughes, Paul Ince and Andrei Kanchelskis – and played a group of players from the Manchester United youth team. The decision was ridiculed in the media, but that season United went on to win the double of the FA Cup and the Premiership. Sir Alex could sense that the environment was changing and that he needed to adapt in order to remain competitive. He also had a solid belief in what

> *An interesting feature of leaders who demonstrate adaptability is the tendency to try the unthinkable*

his youth strategy could achieve. Many great successes are based on ideas that may seem ridiculous initially but, in retrospect, are incredibly simple and effective.

If you consider any environment – business, academic, natural or sporting environments, for example – and compare it to what it was 25 years ago, many elements of the environment would have changed dramatically. Rules and regulations have been reformed and the boundaries have been stretched in different directions. Adaptable leaders

Adaptable leaders are constantly striving to change the rules, almost always for their own benefit, to remain competitive

are constantly striving to change the rules, almost always for their own benefit, to remain competitive.

Manchester United fans will never forget the minutes ticking away in the 1992/93 season in the game against Sheffield Wednesday. Sir Alex was renowned for watching the additional injury time. In this instance, the game went on for seven extra minutes, which was unheard of. Those seven minutes were critical that season, as United turned a score of 0-1 to the opposition into a 2-1 victory. Since then the football authorities have introduced the fourth official, who holds a sign confirming how much extra time will be added. The ironic chants in a United game of 'Fergie time' from rival fans whenever more than a minute or two is added to the regulation 90 minutes are more accurate than the chanting fans probably realise. The Premier League would be loath to admit it, but this is an ideal example of Ferguson's leadership influencing the league's environment.

Great leaders are constantly challenging the status quo, and while it is often for their own benefit, it can serve the greater good in the long term. Currently there is considerable pressure in football to make referees more accountable and to institute the use of goal-line technology. Football's authorities are rightly chided for being slow to change, but the managers' need to adapt will surely create the impetus to sway the authorities into taking the necessary technological steps forward.

It's interesting that managers of small teams always claim that the bigger teams receive preferential treatment from the authorities and referees. This never seemed to bother one of the greatest managers of all time, Brian Clough, the former manager of Nottingham Forest and Derby County, neither of which are considered massive clubs. Clough possessed a unique style of leadership that has never really been repeated, which suggests, perhaps, that the authorities do not favour big clubs, but rather influential leaders!

At this point it's appropriate to mention one of the youth players Sir Alex introduced to the world, the shy, good-looking midfielder discussed briefly in Chapter 2: David Beckham. Beckham first caught the world's attention with an outrageous goal from the halfway line against Wimbledon in 1996, and he's rarely been out of the headlines since. At United, a long and successful spell ended with the infamous flying boot in the United dressing room – Sir Alex kicked a boot in anger and by chance it hit Beckham on the head, symbolically ending their time together.

With England, Beckham's red card in the 1998 World Cup loss to Argentina and his free kick against Greece that saw his country through to the 2002 World Cup represented both ends of the footballing spectrum, from villain to hero. As a footballer he's had considerable success, but it's his ability to adapt and reinvent himself that's most relevant here.

Partly, that applies in a footballing context: following his move to Real Madrid, he learnt Spanish, found his feet in a new and different league, and established himself as one of the club's *Galácticos*. In America, he found himself the celebrity heartbeat of a Los Angeles Galaxy team leading the American quest to reinvent the professional game in the United States. Beckham had to combine football leadership with the role of brand-ambassador-in-chief for LA Galaxy, as well as the game, in America. And it's this last role that leads to the real example he's set in adaptability: completing the transition from shy United trainee to one of the most recognisable faces – and brands – in the world.

Helped by the celebrity status of his wife Victoria, the footballer has driven the Beckham brand into a space that no other footballer has come close to. The commercial distractions that worried Sir Alex at United have become central to the position in which Beckham now finds himself: with his own fragrance, his own line of underwear, and multiple commercial partnerships, deals and endorsements, Beckham has become a wealthy and influential man. And this from the player who started off as an absolute PR disaster.

On being asked in one of his early interviews after having made the first team if he was volatile, he replied that he was – he could play in the centre, and on both the right wing and the left wing! Then, a few weeks later, he was asked what kind of impact his parents had had on his football career. 'They have always been there for me, ever since I was seven,' he replied. So weren't they around before he was seven? To top it all off, when he was asked his thoughts on his manager, Sir Alex, he responded, 'I think he's the best manager I've ever had ... well, he's the only manager I've ever had, but he's the best.' Imagine the field day the comedians and pundits had after those comments.

Yet over time Beckham learnt to think of appropriate replies before speaking and to seek out PR advice, and today he's widely acknowledged as the greatest sports PR person of all time. He is an excellent example of someone who has learnt more about himself and his environment in order to be successful.

His feat of adapting to the football environments in which he has played makes for a notable success story, as is the way he's worked his way into the business world. Combining the two as he has suggests that Beckham is a shrewd, focused individual who is far more than just a winning smile and a great right foot. He's learnt to deal with the media from his public relations team, and he understands the demands of the business world and has created a powerful international brand, all before the age of 40.

> *Beckham is a shrewd, focused individual who is far more than just a winning smile and a great right foot*

I admire the steps Beckham has taken to become so incredibly successful, and I marvel even more at the success of Sir Alex Ferguson. The European game has given us many exceptional managers in recent years, however, and if there is one person who is deserving of particular praise and who warrants mention in this chapter, it's a man who doesn't get the same sort of attention as the Wengers and Mourinhos, the Mancinis and Guardiolas: it is Everton's boss, David Moyes.

Working with a limited budget, modest resources and a player base that has few stars but plenty of committed, hard-working players, Moyes has not only kept Everton in the Premiership, but has got them into Europe, established a consistent presence in the right half of the league table and delighted in bloodying the noses of expensively assembled rivals. As the unforgettable 2011/12 season came to its absurdly dramatic climax, Moyes's team fought back from a 4-2 deficit to earn a 4-4 draw against Manchester United at Old Trafford in what is seen as the game that cost United the title. Equally important is the message it conveyed about Everton – that they are a team of determined players driven on by a furiously committed manager who refuses to concede defeat or relinquish belief in his players.

Moyes exhibits many of the qualities of Sir Alex and has a very similar background, which has led to his being suggested as future manager at Old Trafford. The two Scots also share the ability to adapt; in Moyes we have an exceptional example of a leader stretching, managing and organising his resources to achieve results beyond what could reasonably have been expected. Two key examples drive this home. In the aftermath of Wayne Rooney's departure for United, the prognosis for Everton was grim: with the star of the club's future having gone, Everton was surely reduced to the Premiership fringes, unable to keep top players and thus destined never to pose a serious threat to the established order.

Try telling David Moyes that. He accepted the inevitability of losing Rooney, held out for appropriate compensation and then did what he's done so shrewdly throughout his managerial career: he sought good, value-for-money talent and brought it into his existing squad. He then coaxed out of these players performances that even they might not have imagined they were capable of. Players like Tim Cahill, Mikel Arteta, Phil Neville and Tim Howard, who were all brought into the Everton squad, were among a group of players that has turned Everton from being fringe contenders in the Premiership to a team that consistently punches above its weight. This leads to the second example of Moyes's outstanding leadership: that of my countryman, Steven Pienaar.

An exhilarating player when in full flow, Pienaar possesses the touch, vision and awareness that gives some players that extra second on the ball. But Pienaar is also a slight player, and Moyes could quite easily have dismissed him as too small to handle the Premiership. Instead, he invested faith in a kid from Cape Town who had done well at Ajax Amsterdam but still had a lot to prove. Pienaar quickly became Everton's talisman. In the process, he reminded the football community of how sharp an eye for footballing talent his Scottish manager has.

And that really is the calling card of David Moyes: whether it's a star player supposedly beyond his prime, blue-collar talent that simply needs someone to invest a little belief in it or a burgeoning maestro in search of the right platform, Everton's manager has created a team that has not just adapted to the rough and tumble of Europe's most demanding league, but become a consistent hurdle to English football's top sides.

It is also appropriate at this point to mention the man who broke the hearts of the red half of Manchester at the end of the 2011/12 season, but gave the blue half their biggest cheer in 44 years. (He was also responsible for taking at least 10 years off my life. The astonishing climax to the 2011/12 season vividly illustrated just why the Premiership is such a compelling product with global support.)

Roberto Mancini is in an unenviable position, given Manchester City's newfound Middle Eastern wealth. In theory, the club can go out and buy anyone, but with that sort of financial muscle comes a huge weight of expectation, as well as the risk of a squad full of big-name stars all trying to squeeze into a starting XI. The second of those challenges was Mancini's biggest in what turned out to be a glorious season for City. The running drama surrounding Carlos Tévez and the unpredictable behaviour of Italian striker Mario Balotelli generated the wrong sort of headlines for Mancini, threatening to derail a team that had started the season in spellbinding form.

But Mancini somehow kept his squad in check, refusing to sell Tévez despite the Argentinean doing his best to engineer a final escape from Manchester. He carefully managed the game time of the gifted but volatile Balotelli and, in the end, Tévez returned to help guide City through the final weeks of the league (Balotelli's sparing contributions also chipped in). In 2011/12 Mancini gave a masterclass in adapting to the ego and personality of superstar footballers, a major challenge for the modern manager. His challenge now, of course, is to take that forward and build on the league success.

But there is a hurdle to be cleared with regard to finances, one that will test the adaptability of managers and owners, and one that Chelsea in particular will have to address. New UEFA regulations demand that clubs become more financially stable operations and discontinue the practice of simply writing off huge wage bills and transfer fees as losses at the end of a given season. The wealth of countries like Abu Dhabi and Russia will have to be applied far more judiciously and managed more stringently than it has been to date.

Across Europe, the transfer market will undergo an appreciable change, and managers like Mancini will have to be much more deliberate in the buying and selling of players. In recent years, the bigger clubs have seemed oblivious to the bottom line, an untenable situation in the business world. That is set to change radically.

To sum up, it's the one-sided punch-up with Gordon McQueen that I recall most vividly for the lesson I took away from it and the message I subsequently implemented. Change for the sake of change itself often does little more than upset the equilibrium, but change for the sake of strategic improvement is not only important to both football club and business, but fatal if not carried out. Football's answer to calls for adaptability today is all too often provided in a change of coach or a stream of new players. At United, by contrast, the manager has instilled a culture of adaptability within the existing framework of the club's personnel, with the buying and selling of players never occurring without good reason and the manager always responding to the constant change of the modern football environment.

Change for the sake of strategic improvement is not only important to both football club and business, but fatal if not carried out

Striving to improve the players he works with and seeking those who will complement and enhance his squad is how Sir Alex has remained at the top for as long as he has. It is his humble approach that allows him to accept that he needs to keep learning about himself, his colleagues and his environment, and this leads to one final point that needs to be reaffirmed: hard work is required to make time for learning.

In his biography it is said, 'His [Sir Alex's] appetite for improvement, and self-improvement was gargantuan.' No learning is going to happen without the desire and hunger for success. You know what you have to do to be successful, and if you truly want that success, there is no option but to do it. And it's not just about doing enough, but going the extra mile.

Hard work is required to make time for learning

In my life it was working at the radio station during the day and studying for my MBA at night that eventually led to my creating a successful living. Once you're on your feet, it then becomes crucial not only to keep improving, but to inspire colleagues and teammates to improve. One of Sir Alex's former players at Aberdeen, Mark McGhee, came into the dressing room expecting a pat on the back after making four goals in a match. Instead he received flak for not passing the ball more often. 'It was the things you weren't good at that he [Sir Alex] would keep urging you to improve. He wanted to see improvement in a player.'

Sir Alex has had myriad opportunities to rest on his laurels, but he never has. It's a lesson in sustained excellence and application that cannot be ignored.

TRAINING DAY

There are two kinds of adaptability: personal adaptability, and that pertaining to an organisation or team. The key feature of being an adaptable leader is having the courage to make timely, sometimes unpopular, decisions. This means that the leader has to be very clear about what he or she wants to achieve. In addition, adaptability is about possessing and enacting the conviction that there is no such thing as failure; there is only opportunity to learn. To develop this attitude, try the following:

> *The key feature of being an adaptable leader is having the courage to make timely, sometimes unpopular, decisions*

1. Identify situations where you have delayed making decisions. Why were these decisions delayed – was it due to a lack of clarity or fear of the outcome? Who were the key stakeholders involved in the outcome of the decisions? What are your feelings towards these stakeholders?

2. Identify situations where you have made timely decisions. What were your reasons for making these decisions? Who were the key stakeholders involved in the outcome of the decisions, and how do you feel towards these stakeholders?

3. What process of problem solving do you adopt when making decisions? Do you feel you need all questions answered before committing to a decision? Do you feel comfortable making assumptions? Does this vary for different types of decisions?

4. Adopt the following simple framework, which will help in creating adaptability:

    a. Learn about yourself (self-awareness) – refer back to your reflections at the end of Chapter 3 to understand why you feel the way you do in certain situations.

    b. Learn about others (observation) – refer back to your reflections at the end of Chapter 3 to understand how people react in different situations.

    c. Learn about your environment – understand the nature of the world in which you operate and how it is changing. Take courses and don't stop asking questions.

FULL-TIME TAKEAWAY

- Ensure that you have an appetite to learn and improve constantly.
- Limit your ego so that you accept there is much you need to learn.
- Learn about yourself, your colleagues and your environment, and always be prepared to adapt appropriately.
- Accept that you will sometimes have to make untimely and unpopular decisions and, if they go wrong, be willing to learn and to try again.

5

Dreams and Destiny

'Dream as if you'll live forever,
live as if you'll die tomorrow.'
– James Dean

If you'd asked me 40 years ago where I would end up today, I'd have spoken excitedly of being an astronaut or a policeman. I might also have mentioned football, and winning a World Cup after scoring the deciding goal. But, like jetting off into space or chasing bank robbers across town, sirens blaring, football was a vague, hope-filled fantasy, and while it morphed into a clear vision of intent as I got older, there is no way I could seriously have told you as a teenager that I would end up at a World Cup and play at the level of football that I eventually did.

Dreams of playing professional football grew as I discovered my aptitude for the game. A sense of aspiration and ambition fuelled the talent I had and drove me to practise harder, train longer and do everything I could to translate my potential into footballing success, and my dream into reality.

It is important not to misconstrue the word 'dream'. The Disneyesque interpretation of today has given a fairy-tale aspect to dreams, instilling in them a sense of the unattainable. But the most satisfying dreams also require an element of realism: playing for Manchester United wasn't complete fantasy for me, as I did have talent as a footballer. By contrast, anyone who's seen me on the golf course would know that dreams of winning the Open Championship would have been extremely far-flung. The opening quote sums up so much of what this chapter aims to convey. It's about creating an exciting and attainable dream, and then striving towards it with energy, passion and commitment.

Professor Sondhi discusses below the departure point for creating dreams that can, in time, become destiny:

The challenge for all individuals is to believe in what is attainable. Sometimes we may sell ourselves short, opting for an easier way out – one that doesn't demand we move out of our comfort zones. Alternatively, setting a goal that is clearly beyond our capabilities is likely to be destructive. Crucial to the creation and realisation of goals is an individual's stage of development. In football, many clubs recruit children at the age of seven and discard others, failing to consider older football hopefuls. This ignores the fact that potential often emerges later in life. It is important to establish how realistic a certain dream is and to assess at what stage of the individual's life or business he or she will be able to implement

> *The challenge for all individuals is to believe in what is attainable*

that dream. Above all, the person must believe that he or she can turn the dream into destiny.

Playing first for United and later for England did deliver on my schoolboy fantasies: running out for United on my debut was a surreal occasion, and I don't remember much beyond the excitement, the nerves and the nagging suspicion that somehow it couldn't all be real. My debut, which came a lot earlier than I'd expected, materialised more through circumstance than through my blowing away the manager with my goalkeeping prowess.

Manchester United had been looking to sign Jim Blyth after the first-team keeper, Paddy Roche, had had a nightmare and let five goals in during an away match at Birmingham. One of the players mentioned to me that he'd heard the deal with Jim was off because he had a dodgy back, and the doctors wouldn't give their consent for him to be signed. I knew that two of our keepers were injured and one was sick, which left me. When our manager, Dave Sexton, called me over, I was expecting him to say something really special and build me up. Instead, he gave me one of the great motivational speeches of all time: 'Gary, we've got NO other goalkeepers available, so you're playing tomorrow against Ipswich.' That was it.

But it was still my debut, regardless of the path that had led me to the number-one jersey. Playing against the town of my birth, we beat Ipswich 2-0 at Old Trafford to get my career off to the ideal start. Although my memories of that day are hazy, the crowd singing 'There's only one Gary Bailey!' was electrifying, and I remember thinking that whatever else happened in my life, I'd played for Manchester United and that was something I'd always have.

Unfortunately, I remember my England debut with far greater, colder clarity. Peter Shilton had been rested, handing me my big opportunity. Playing against Ireland at Wembley, Liam Brady got in a shot and, to my horror (I still remember it in painful slow motion), the ball squeezed under me and into the goal. I can still hear the England fans singing 'There's only one Peter Shilton!' as I write this. Goalkeeping can be a cruel job.

Much as I get no pleasure from that particular moment, it was one of many that confirmed the greatest lesson I've taken from the game of football: my destiny was, and continues to be, in my own hands. There's a great Gwyneth Paltrow movie, *Sliding Doors*, where the lead character makes a simple decision that changes the outcome of her life. There are two possible paths from that crucial point, and the movie follows both of them, showing how a single moment can change the course of your life.

> *My destiny was, and continues to be, in my own hands*

My 'sliding door' moment was my first year at a new high school, Rondebosch Boys' High School in Cape Town. My dad had been made manager of Cape Town City soccer team and he wanted me to go to Rondebosch, one of the city's top schools. The only free places, however, were in the art and woodwork stream – not my strengths! I had always got firsts for maths and not much else, but I attended the school all the same. At the end of that year (Grade 10), the school held tests to see who had the ability to move up to the maths and science stream (the brains). A friend and I decided to have a go at the tests, but on the day he pulled out, so I decided to do likewise.

But after giving it some thought, I realised that I would never forgive myself for not trying – I would rather try and fail – so I wrote the tests. Although I was expecting dismal marks, I was happy that I'd at least made the effort. To my pleasant surprise (and my dad's amazement), I sailed through, moved up to the top stream and eventually went to Wits University to study engineering. (My incredibly funny Manchester United teammates called it 'Half-Wits University'. It never failed to amuse them.)

Everyone has that 'sliding door' moment, and it's up to you not to have regrets. Try something (as long as you feel you have the ability), and then enjoy the success – or, at worst, learn from the failure, knowing that you gave it your best shot.

There are always external factors over which you have no control

There are always external factors over which you have no control. For a footballer, injury is the obvious one. But how you respond to difficult situations, and what you make of the opportunities you have, defines your future. Responding to challenging situations requires a couple of things. First, you need to find strength internally to get through the immediate situation – this is the professional will mentioned earlier. There is little point in looking to the future if you can't get through the present. Reframing, as discussed in Chapter 1, is the ideal way to get this challenge into a balanced and positive perspective.

When you find the strength to get through the present, you can set off on the road to the destiny you've envisioned

Second, you need to have a goal, a dream of what the future can look like. When you find the strength to get through the present, you can set off on the road to the destiny you've envisioned. There is an added aspect to professional will, reframing and creating a dream, and that is to have a strategy or plan.

One of the most challenging periods of my life was my divorce, an intensely stressful time that, sadly, a lot of people go through. It isn't necessary to elaborate on the reasons for it here; what is relevant is that by the time you read this, I'll be married again – to a former Miss Universe! My mates are convinced she'll come to her senses before then; they can't believe that I've made good on that classic schoolboy dream of marrying a supermodel.

Michelle McLean was crowned Miss Universe in 1992 and was someone I'd only ever seen on television and magazine covers. Before I met her, I'd been single for six years and had met many wonderful and delightful women during that time. For a few years, however, I had felt the desire to settle down and enjoy the permanent company of someone special. My previous girlfriends had all wanted kids and I hadn't, but we'd still dated. This was an incredibly dumb strategic move for an MBA graduate. In the middle of each of these relationships it became a huge deal-breaker, as I obviously wasn't going to settle down with any of them if we had different expectations with respect to children.

So I decided to write a list of what I wanted from a woman, keeping it as short as possible. It went something along the lines of: beautiful, wonderful person, intelligent, doesn't want kids ... Writing down my desires helped me to attain clarity on what I should be focusing on while looking for a partner. The first person to whom I mentioned my list suggested that Michelle might fit those criteria.

When I did eventually meet her, she turned out to be warm, funny and intelligent – and she was the very first person I'd considered since drawing up my new strategy. (By the way, since meeting, she's also vastly improved her understanding of the offside law, and can't understand why André Villas-Boas dropped Frank Lampard from the Chelsea starting XI.) My destiny to marry a Miss Universe?

It wouldn't have happened without the focus provided by a simple, logical plan.

Both Sir Alex Ferguson and José Mourinho understand the importance of meticulous planning. Andy Roxburgh, the UEFA technical director and former Scotland manager, says: 'Mourinho leaves the absolute minimum to chance – he does have that instinct for the game, but prefers to do as much as possible through preparation.' Similarly, Sir Alex has said that the key to a winning mentality and achieving your dreams is 'a will to win, and attention to detail'.

Sir Alex has said that the key to a winning mentality and achieving your dreams is 'a will to win, and attention to detail'

The definition of a dream is important. Separating wild, hopeful aspirations from the more specific ambitions that may be possible contextualises destiny, what it means and how much control we really have over it. It's a fundamental issue in achieving success under pressure, and one that Professor Sondhi addresses here:

Dreams are images that engage our emotions, representing a future desired state – such as Sir Alex's dream for the youth team that he turned into an all-conquering first XI. This vision was built on a simple plan. Sir Alex didn't have the money to buy a great team, so he had to build one, and he designed a plan to find players who would bring the glory, starting with the Premiership title and ultimately becoming England's most consistently successful club.

These dreams are deeply associated with our emotions, which is why they can be so powerful, but some people's dreams are actually nothing more than wishes. The attainable varies from one person to another. People will have a number of dreams or wishes in addition to having priorities. As we get older, these dreams begin to become more tangible, but they also become more measured – marrying a Miss Universe goes out the window (unless you're Gary) as we dream instead of health and education for our children, for instance. It's vital, therefore, that we distinguish between dreams that are merely wishful and a destiny that can be achieved – which, in turn, depends on application of the right values and practices, along with hard work, dedication, adaptability and commitment.

> *It's vital that we distinguish between dreams that are merely wishful and a destiny that can be achieved*

Players like Cristiano Ronaldo, David Beckham and Éric Cantona may look like complete naturals on the field, but every one of them was famous at Old Trafford for training harder than anyone else. Gary's teammate Lou Macari speaks of how dedicated Gary was in training and how he often used to spend twice as much time training as others, something that kept him in the number-one jersey for so long.

Dreams create a desire for something that, at the time, may seem impossible. The dream makes the brain very adaptive, however, and as we envision it more clearly and become more comfortable with it, so our horizons broaden, our belief takes shape and what had previously seemed impossible starts to appear possible. We find solutions to the blockages that hindered us initially and build the determination to push past those obstacles. If we do not visualise our destiny, then it is unlikely to happen.

> *Dreams create a desire for something that, at the time, may seem impossible*

At an organisational level, dreams are represented by the vision of the company, where it wants to be. Sir Alex's vision and Manchester United's vision appear to be the same thing, but in fact they are the interwoven destinies of two different but complementary sets of dreams.

Although destiny suggests a predetermined course of events, this is not accurate. Motivational speakers who insist that you can be anything you want to be regardless of your circumstances are usually wrong, but you *can* be anything you want to be, provided that you possess the basic ingredients with regard to capability and are prepared to overcome the challenges that will hinder your progress. While some things can't be changed, many can, and understanding what these are and how to manage them are intrinsic to creating your own destiny rather than passively waiting to see what that destiny might be.

Great leaders have a deep appreciation of the factors that drive their vision, and they know how to build on these factors. Sir Alex, from day one, had a deep understanding of how to deliver performance. He decided that what was needed to achieve long-term success was a strong, well-funded youth system, the subsequent products of which are now the stuff of Old Trafford legend. He also had an unwavering belief in his philosophy. Note that this doesn't imply inflexibility in approach – as discussed in the previous chapter, adaptability is key to Sir Alex's philosophy and therefore to his belief system.

If you consider visionary leaders in business, you often get a sense that they happen to make the right decisions at the right

> *At an organisational level, dreams are represented by the vision of the company, where it wants to be*

times, but these leaders possess a strong vision that provides a unique focus on the situation. Thus, what appear to be snappy decisions with fortuitous outcomes are in reality the carefully thought-out steps of a clear plan.

Dreams become destiny as a result of a number of factors. While not everyone can win the 100-metre gold medal or a Nobel Prize, we have far more control over our own destinies than we tend to realise. All the football leaders discussed in this book have possessed a strong belief that they can deliver in the face of adversity. This is a key characteristic of successful leaders and indicates the professional will needed to rise to the top.

When things are looking bleak and dreams are being challenged, the visionary leader possesses the conviction that change is not only possible, but probable

This belief is further enhanced through gratitude and the reframing of challenges, which provide the enthusiasm and energy that fuel a dream and turn it into destiny. When things are looking bleak and dreams are being challenged, the visionary leader possesses the conviction that change is not only possible, but probable – and expresses gratitude for the chance to make that change happen.

My personal dreams – to become the number-one goalkeeper for one of the world's biggest football teams and to play for England – were as simple as Sir Alex's, and no less bold. With these dreams in mind, I undertook a crazy trip in 1984, while United were in Australia for an off-season tour. The tour coincided with the European Under-21 Championship in England, and Sir Bobby Robson wanted me to take my place in goals in the England side for the final. But my club manager, Ron Atkinson, wanted me to stay in Australia for the tour and play over the weekend. I checked flights and found out that I could fly back, play for England in the final against Spain, and get back to Australia in time for United's match. When I asked Ron, he was furious, saying that I had club dinners to attend, that we had already lost our senior England players and that I was one of the star attractions. It was decision-time for me, and it was tough.

I upset Ron by deciding to play in both games. I knew that my goal was to play for England at the highest level, and missing the final of the European Under-21 Championship would damage that dream. We won the final, the only other senior trophy won by England apart from the 1966 World Cup. Two years later, when Sir Bobby Robson included me in the 1986 World Cup squad despite carrying an injury, he made reference to the commitment I'd shown to the Under-21 side in flying back from Australia.

Playing regularly for England was a rather optimistic dream, given that I was playing in the era of Ray Clemence and Peter Shilton, two of the finest keepers the game has ever seen. But both of my dreams drove me to work furiously, to train flat out and to commit everything I had to becoming both Manchester United and England's goalkeeper. After 373 games for United and a World Cup for England, I reckon the hard work paid off.

The important thing here, as in so much of life, is balance. On the one hand, if you set yourself too outrageous a set of goals, the failure to translate them into reality will only get you down. But, on the other, if you don't extend your vision and push your own boundaries, you'll never make the most of the potential that you or your business have to offer. The balance, then, is finding the dream that's on the horizon and then driving yourself or your business towards it. The dream is the first step to the reality that you want your future to hold, which leads to your destiny. Thus, as Professor Sondhi pointed out, the two work hand in hand.

> *The balance is finding the dream that's on the horizon and then driving yourself or your business towards it*

Rather than pin a wild dream on the wall of his office and hope that he'd get there one day, Sir Alex realised that only one person could engineer his destiny: Alex Ferguson. He set about building the team that was eventually to usurp Liverpool's position as the most successful team in England. Now into his seventies, Sir Alex is still at the top. As Professor Sondhi explains, this was, and continues to be, the crux of Sir Alex's success:

> *Sir Alex realised that only one person could engineer his destiny: Alex Ferguson*

Sir Alex's personal dream was to be the best manager he could be. He needed a vision that would excite and engage the key stakeholders – the supporters. He also recognised that, to achieve this dream, he needed to be successful for a sustained period rather than for just a couple of years. United had fallen so far behind the competition that getting to the top was not going to be a quick or easy job. Sir Alex's understanding of this was essential to turning the dream into his, and United's, destiny.

Winners are able to turn their dreams into destiny by understanding what's driving them, where they want to be and what's needed to get there. They are fully aware of their passions and the factors that drive those passions, and successful leaders follow their passions. Following a passion ensures that you never give up when times get tough and forces you to pay attention to the details that differentiate those who are successful from those who are not. Planning and passion provide extra energy and the focus to deliver the desired outcome.

So how can Sir Alex's approach be translated into a set of guidelines for the achievement of personal or business goals? At the core of

Winners are able to turn their dreams into destiny by understanding what's driving them, where they want to be and what's needed to get there

what the United boss did was planning and investing in a future he believed in, which facilitated the emergence of an extraordinary group of young footballers. David Beckham, Paul Scholes, Nicky Butt, Ryan Giggs and the Neville brothers were young, talented and, as commentators gleefully pointed out as they wrote off the hopes of a young United side, woefully short on experience. It wasn't too long before exactly the same commentators were loudly proclaiming that they'd always known Ferguson's young team would succeed.

The question is how to find the time, in an increasingly pressurised and frantic business environment, to plan carefully for the future, and to create dreams that will lead you to success. The answer, for me, has everything to do with fitness and health. Recently the Harvard Business School's magazine made special reference to how much extra activity the modern business person is having to cope with – emails, text messages and social media, to name but a few. The time spent on these things had to come from somewhere, and generally it was coming from the periods normally allocated to forward planning, dreaming and creating long-term strategies. One of the ways to make more time is to keep healthy and increase your energy levels so that you can complete your primary work in less time and so free up some planning time.

The body is an engine, and generally people don't look after their bodies, but, as Sir Alex said in an interview with Alistair Campbell, 'If you have physical fitness, you have mental fitness.' Manchester United legend Bryan Robson told me that he'd always been amazed by how Sir Alex still found time to exercise, even into his late sixties. I don't have time to get to the gym every day, so I've set up my treadmill opposite the television. When I watch football, I try to get in my 30-minute run, which I do three times a week. Add to that a few weights while watching the game and plenty of stretches before and after, and I've managed to combine my enjoyment of watching football with my desire to keep myself as fit and healthy as I possibly can, and to do so with minimum use of valuable time.

My GP has told me that men in particular need to be careful of putting on weight, because we are not built to carry extra weight as women are (due to pregnancy). Being anything over 10 per cent of your normal weight carries the risk of heart attack, especially as you get older.

A major destroyer of energy and productivity is emotional conflict. In order to address this, identify the two or three emotional situations that get you most upset. Write them down and spend time appraising why they affect you and how you can nullify the impact that they have. By knowing how to deal with situations that get you worked up and increase your stress levels, you cut down on distractions, reduce stress and increase your overall health. It's not foolproof, though – I still haven't quite mastered the art of calmly

A major destroyer of energy and productivity is emotional conflict

accepting referee decisions, even from the neutral distance of the television studio ...

There's also merit in taking time to consider emotional responses in business, particular when it comes to today's primary medium of communication: email. An irate response or a throwaway line in a phone call is easier to dismiss than a similar inclusion in an email, which is a tangible record. When you've written an email invested with strong emotion of any sort – a complaint, a criticism, a threat to resign – try to leave that email in your inbox for an hour, as I've mentioned before, and then come back to it, reread it and make sure you haven't let emotion cloud your judgement. It's a simple approach, but one that can save you a lot of awkward, embarrassing or confrontational situations, and will almost certainly lower the prospect of making enemies in your working environment.

There are many ways to address the challenge of trying to fit so much into each day. Whenever I allow the stress to overwhelm me and lapse into a moment of self-pity, I think of a Scotsman in his seventies in Manchester who runs the world's most successful football club, manages some of the biggest egos in sport, oversees the flow of talent in and out of his squad, deals with intense media scrutiny on a daily basis, and still has time to keep an eye on his racehorses, collect red wine, spend time with his family and indulge his interest in gardening.

Proving people wrong has become a speciality of Sir Alex's, but the more important point to focus on is the planning that went into being able to prove them wrong. Knowing where he wanted to be and what he needed to do to get there was the result of time spent evaluating his dream for Manchester United and the road that would lead him to it.

Sir Alex has also proved a master at keeping the processes by which he operates as simple and as efficient as possible. In the *Harvard Business Review* of April 2012, Walter Isaacson writes about Apple founder Steve Jobs and the leadership lessons he left us with: 'Jobs's Zenlike ability to focus was accompanied by the related instinct to simplify things by zeroing in on their essence and eliminating unnecessary components.'

While Apple and United may offer two very different products, the similarity in leadership style between Jobs and Sir Alex is considerable. Planning in an efficient, focused manner enabled both men to mould their destinies and those of their organisations in turn. Often, though, destiny is not set in stone, as Professor Sondhi points out:

A key feature of Sir Alex's United dream was that he constantly reviewed it, which shaped his subsequent actions accordingly. The perfect starting XI only stays that way for a certain period – players get injured, retire, or lose form or focus. Ambition changes as well: overtaking Liverpool's title haul might have been the overarching goal, but cup victories, success in Europe and the ability to attract big-name players all grew more important as United became re-established as one of England's top clubs. In essence, then, creating your destiny demands flexibility and an understanding of when your goals have to change as you move closer to the destiny you're trying to fulfil.

Sir Alex did a couple of important things in this regard that are worth repeating. First, he made his goal public: overtake Liverpool. Yes, it takes courage (particularly if it's a claim like that), but once your goal is in the public domain, the drive to make it happen becomes that much stronger. You or your business might not have the back pages of the *Sun* and the *Mirror* reminding you of your goal on a weekly basis, but if you've announced to your industry, your competitors and/or your peers that you want to achieve something in particu- lar, their awareness of your stated dream is a powerful motivator. It's here that self-belief and confidence allow you to commit to something that might sound out- rageous to the rest of the world (and, at times,

If you've announced to your industry, your competitors and/ or your peers that you want to achieve something in particular, their awareness of your stated dream is a powerful motivator

to yourself). You may be uncertain about the goal on occasion, but you need to push yourself that little bit further to achieve it, and eventually doing this becomes a habit.

Second, Sir Alex didn't say that he wanted to be the best, a common fault in the formulation of dreams, goals and ambitions. 'Best' is a wonderfully vague term; had things not gone right for United, Sir Alex could easily have gone back and, with a little spin, laid claim to the best development, or defence, or home record, or any number of spurious claims that wouldn't, technically, have been untrue. Instead, he wanted to overtake Liverpool, a clearly stated, specific dream that invited no misinterpretation or mis- understanding of what he wanted to achieve.

Set the same specific goal for your business or your personal horizon. Do you want your company to have the biggest market share? Your product to sell a million units? Your brand to be seen in 20 different countries? Whatever the target you set yourself, clearly define it: you know exactly what you need to do to make good on it. Do that, and breezy ambitions of being the 'best' fall away.

Third, understand and appreciate your goal before you tell the world what it is. Chasing down Liverpool made for an emotional call to arms for United, but it wasn't simple rhetoric – there's always something more to Sir Alex when he makes calls he knows will be headlines the following morning. In this instance, he'd

Understand and appreciate your goal before you tell the world what it is

worked out that winning the number of titles required to overtake the league's most successful team was a tough but achievable target. He knew it would take an enormous amount of work, and that getting there could take a decade or more – but he believed that it was achievable.

He also understood that with every title knocked off in pursuit of Liverpool, he'd be creating individual moments of success that would not only draw United closer to Liverpool's benchmark, but also sustain the constant thirst for achievement that's endemic to professional sport.

Finally, there's the power of the dream that Sir Alex created, a dream that gathered momentum as United's success took shape. Simply having a goal can become a narrow objective, focused to the point of blocking out anything else. The dream engages your senses and encourages a broader, more balanced approach to creating your own future rather than waiting for it to come into view.

Had Sir Alex simply said that he wanted to win 10 titles in the next two decades, he'd never have invoked the passion of supporters and opponents the way he did by setting Liverpool so firmly in his sights. Tapping into the imagination of the English game gave his dream an energy that did much to sustain his guidance of United towards their subsequent success. As Professor Sondhi suggests, this offers a valuable pointer for the business world.

There is generally a lack of engagement of the senses in the setting of dreams, goals and visions in the corporate world. Pick up a newspaper for a simple comparison in this respect. Read a match report on a big game in any sport, and you'll have a piece of writing invested with the emotion of the match in question. If you flick to the financial pages of the same newspaper and read a report responding to a company's results, you'll find a far more serious article. Granted, the discrepancies reflect fundamental differences with regard to content and presumed readership, but they also subscribe to an image of the corporate world that's not necessarily accurate. Business doesn't have to be grey suits, dull speeches and the soulless crunching of numbers: some of the most successful leaders in recent times, such as Sir Richard Branson or Steve Jobs, have led with flair and excitement.

And so that ubiquitous vision statement, 'To be the number one or two in our selected markets ...', needs to change. This type of vision lacks any emotional content and consequently is very difficult for stakeholders to embrace. If you want to inspire your employees, investors or customers, follow Sir Alex's example and settle on a bold but attainable vision that speaks to the heart of those people whom you want to have listen to you or buy into your idea. Trade in the generic mission statement for one that invokes real excitement. You'll need to evaluate yourself, your company or your product to work out what that is, but, as Sir Alex has illustrated, a dream with more than one believer becomes that much easier to reach.

> *Business doesn't have to be grey suits, dull speeches and the soulless crunching of numbers*

There is another crucial element to dreams and the creation of destiny that often gets lost in the excitement of having a dream. I love this quote of Nolan Bushnell's: 'Everyone who's ever taken a shower has an idea. It's the person who gets out of the shower, dries off, and does something about it who makes a difference.' We've all got the girl, scored the winning goal, written the perfect novel in the sanctuary of the shower – and then gone off to work, dreams shelved for another day. That tomorrow's success depends on today's planning is no great revelation, but investing time in planning and preparation is something we simply don't do enough of – especially when you consider that, in investing that time, you are creating your destiny.

> *Investing time in planning and preparation is something we simply don't do enough of*

Ken Allen, the CEO of DHL Express, makes the following recommendation: 'Create a profitable business that continuously reinvests, in order to create business sustainability.' This is his plan, simply laid out and easy to follow. The hard bit is getting the commitment from the whole team to make it happen, and of course implementing it, but none of that would follow without having the plan in the first place.

Something that Sir Alex probably didn't figure on was that he would shape more than just his own destiny and that of Manchester United and the players: he would also influence the nature of the professional game today. The significance of winning the treble in 1999 has already been discussed, but it is important that we re-emphasise it here: if Sir Alex had Liverpool's benchmark in his sights when he arrived at Old Trafford, so Europe's big clubs now have Manchester United's extraordinary haul of three major trophies in one season as the ideal target for every new manager.

The bar has been lifted in terms of potential achievement, and as a result new managers have even less scope for failure than they might have had in the past. In order to determine their own destiny, they have to be even more successful, and in a shorter time frame – and that can be linked to Sir Alex's success at Old Trafford.

The lifting of the bar is not limited to United's manager, however. Pep Guardiola's run at Barcelona set the benchmark for European performance, José Mourinho's success in the big three leagues is a magnificent

The bar has been lifted in terms of potential achievement, and as a result new managers have even less scope for failure than they might have had in the past

achievement (as he'll happily point out to you ...), and every success a manager enjoys at a particular club pushes the boundaries of what fans and owners believe their club to be capable of. Mourinho's broaching of the 100-point mark in La Liga, Lionel Messi's staggering haul of 73 goals in 2011/12 – these achievements force those who follow to seek improvement on levels of excellence and thus broaden the scope of their destinies.

Sir Alex's own path involved recognising, nurturing and believing in the talent he had, but also aligning himself with the right coaches and scouts at Old Trafford, establishing relationships with his players, watching and learning from his opponents, and constantly building an understanding of what was needed to achieve the success he craved. Professor Sondhi discusses these below.

A hallmark of Sir Alex and of great leaders in many environments is the importance of their values and belief system to their conviction that the dream can indeed become destiny. These values and beliefs do not allow such leaders to lose sight of the vision they've created. Another factor that drives the ability to turn the dream into destiny is that these leaders are fully 'authentic'.

'Authenticity' is a term used a lot in leadership to describe the degree to which a leader will adapt to fit in with a specific environment. We have mentioned that adaptability is key to success, but the flip side to this is that it should not compromise an individual's identity or values and beliefs. Authentic leaders know exactly what gets them excited and what doesn't, allowing them to decide how adaptable they can and should be.

Consider Arsène Wenger: he sticks closely to the factors most important to him and is clearly very authentic. In particular, he maintains his allegiance to the playing of beautiful football and the development of the bigger picture. While that is highly commendable from an aesthete's perspective, it sometimes appears to compromise his team's ability to win matches.

In addition, Wenger himself has said that his vision for Arsenal is to further the 'Arsenalisation' of the Emirates stadium. He wants to make it the centre of London, building up and developing it as a business rather than simply a football ground. As a result of this, many Arsenal fans may feel that his vision is moving outside his realm of control and is having a negative impact on his performance.

Contrast that with Sir Alex, who is firmly focused on winning and competitiveness. Bill George writes in *Authentic Leadership* that 'authentic leaders demonstrate a passion for their purpose, practice their values consistently, and lead with their hearts as well as their heads. They establish long-term, meaningful relationships and have the self-discipline to get results.' That's quite a combination to get right. As a set of leadership guidelines, it is an ideal summary.

I'm not sure there's anyone on the planet who has better time-management skills than Sir Alex, and the key to that is his energy levels. Once again, this points to the importance of health and fitness, as discussed earlier. Cutting down on muffins and coffee and really looking after your body can give you the energy to ensure you have the time to

Authentic leaders demonstrate a passion for their purpose, practice their values consistently, and lead with their hearts as well as their heads

think about tomorrow, not just today. In tandem with exercise, you can create an astonishing difference in your energy levels: look at the diet and energy regime of South African golfer Gary Player, now well into his seventies but still travelling the world each week and capable of doing one-armed push-ups! That is not something I'm able to manage, and I'm nearly 20 years younger. That we now need to spend so much time planning our activities sums up the nature of the beast that is time management. Professor Sondhi expands on the conundrum:

When coaching people on the importance of time management, I remember considering the various tools designed to help people manage the highly valuable 24 hours of their day (a complete industry was made out of Filofaxes!). I decided that employing a Filofax amounted to little more than writing down a wish list in an expensive leather cover. At this point I created a simple acronym to help with making the most of one's time – DOPE.

The 'D' stands for **discipline**: do what you said you were going to do. People know what they should be doing, but will find excuses for why these things cannot be done. Successful individuals possess the discipline to complete tasks as planned. Sir Alex is renowned for going into the office at seven o'clock every morning, before anyone else gets in. His discipline has created winning habits that anyone is capable of (despite the amazement with which people regard them). Swap procrastination for productivity, and you'll be surprised at what you can accomplish.

People know what they should be doing, but will find excuses for why these things cannot be done. Successful individuals possess the discipline to complete tasks as planned

The 'O' is for **organisation**. By organising different tasks and resources, you will be able to maximise the impact of your disciplined actions. In the blur of demands that make up any given day, it's all too easy for clutter to distract from effective endeavour. Whether it's clearing out your inbox or delegating work you'd like to do but feel can be managed by someone else, having a clear focus of what you need to do and what can be done without you recalibrates your day with surprising effect.

The 'P' stands for **prioritisation**. Prioritising the actions that are needed is probably the most vital factor in shaping the destiny you want. With a clear vision, greater focus on key actions is possible. Redecorating the office lobby might make it look great and be a fun project, but renovating your warehouse to improve delivery efficiencies might be more important.

The 'E' is for **execution**, or carrying out what you have said you are going to do. Successful individuals are consistently one step ahead; the guys they've beaten always seem to have a good reason for why they didn't execute as promised. The successful leader delivers – or, in the context of this chapter, moulds and creates the destiny that's been envisioned. In essence, successful people make things happen rather than wait for them to happen.

A nice, simple acronym to remember – but, as was the case with anything Professor Sondhi suggested I research while doing my MBA, not always so easy to deliver on. But then that's why the successful leader is the exception rather than the rule.

There is another element that's essential to succeeding under pressure. It's one that gives you the platform from which to address the day-to-day challenges of leadership: spiritual welfare, something that we tend to gloss over. You don't have to spend a month doing yoga and eating lentils to look after your spiritual welfare, but you do need to realise that a person in good, positive spirits has the clear mind that is conducive to successful time management and planning.

> *A person in good, positive spirits has the clear mind that is conducive to successful time management and planning*

The clutter of work, relationships, financial demands and general stress can leak into all facets of life. It's human nature for this to happen to an extent, but attempting to compartmentalise the different emotional aspects of your life is crucial. As goalkeeper I couldn't let a missed cross or a fumbled shot play on my mind for too long, just as Sir Alex can't let a defeat haunt him; we all have to learn to accept when things don't go our way, and move on.

One of the tools I've incorporated into my daily routine in attempting to achieve this is to switch off my phone when I'm five minutes from home at the end of the day. Instead I spend that time thinking about the family waiting for me when I get there. It's a simple but effective way of leaving the office behind, switching off from the demands of the working world and focusing on the important people in my life.

Perhaps it's the calming world of gardening that has helped Sir Alex to keep his balance, or the diversion of his racehorses, or the family life that he guards so closely. Most likely it's a combination of the above which allows him the balance that has afforded him the energy and commitment to plan his ascent to the pinnacle of world football.

TRAINING DAY

Dreams demand a high level of self-awareness. You need to know what is important to you and what gets you excited. Intense honesty is required to establish your personal desires and priorities, because sometimes we can end up pursuing someone else's dream. This focus eliminates the need for lots of different goals and priorities and is dependent on the authenticity of the individual. Is your dream really your dream? Is it your priority? Does it get you excited and is it something you feel passionate about? These are the questions to ask in defining and achieving your destiny. Compare your dream to your key values and beliefs and explore the fit between the two. If the fit is poor, then the dream may not be your true dream. To turn the dream into reality, ensure that you provide ample time for reflection on your dreams and their relevance to your current state, and to plan the process of achieving your dreams.

To help you implement the ideas expressed in this chapter, carry out the following five exercises:

1. Write down the things that get you excited. In as much detail as possible, describe why they excite you.
2. Write down your dream. Engage your senses as you describe it, writing it as if you can touch and feel it. Make your description as clear and as detailed as possible.

3. List your key values and beliefs. Ask yourself what is important to you, and be as descriptive as possible.
4. Compare your dream to your values and beliefs. Does your dream fit in with them? How does the dream make you feel? Does the dream take you outside your comfort zone? How does this make you feel? Do you feel energised, or does this worry you?
5. What are your first steps to making your dreams come true? What resources do you need? Do you have these resources?

FULL-TIME TAKEAWAY
1. Dreams should be exciting and attainable, but should stretch you – at least give them a try so that you have no regrets.
2. Dreams become destiny when you follow a plan with dedication, energy and hard work.
3. You can increase your energy levels through regular exercise and healthy eating. This will help you to free up time to plan towards your dream.
4. Using DOPE will assist you in creating an effective plan. Don't underestimate the importance of adding excitement and emotion to your personal or business dream or vision.
5. Reduce stress by understanding your emotional triggers and so manage carefully your responses to friends, family, colleagues or customers.
6. You can reduce stress even further by looking after your spiritual well-being and using techniques to help you focus and prioritise.

6

Support

'There is no other team like them …
The manager expects you to work
hard and win games. It is instilled into
you at a very young age … There is
a never-say-die attitude. It's what
Manchester United have.'
– David Beckham

There are certain people, depending on how a match has gone, whom you don't want to see after 90 minutes: the manager, if you've just lost a game; your goalkeeper, if you're the player who hit the weak back pass that led to the winning goal; and opposition supporters, if you've just been beaten on the road. But the worst person of all to corner you after a match is the defender who's scored the winning goal: you will never, ever hear the end of it.

I'm reminded of this frequently by Lucas Radebe, the former Leeds United and South Africa captain, and one of the modern game's finer defenders. Radebe scored only three times for Leeds, but one of those was vital: a header five minutes from time in a UEFA Cup game that saw Leeds beat Spartak Moscow on the away-goals rule. There's a clip of it on YouTube; I suspect the majority of views logged stem from Radebe himself, dragging unsuspecting dinner guests off to his computer at home, saying, 'There's something I must show you ...'

But for all the fun to be had at the expense of defenders scoring goals, I still get goosebumps when Radebe recalls the aftermath of that goal, because it's something I can identify with. As the ball hit the back of the net, Elland Road erupted in a roar of unrestrained Yorkshire delight. Overcome with nostalgia every time he thinks back to that moment, Lucas insists that he's never heard anything approaching the sheer volume of noise that the Leeds supporters produced when their South African skipper scored that night. It's a memory that captures the delight of playing professional football: hearing your supporters in full cry, celebrating a goal, cheering a victory or simply urging their team on.

Beyond a player's personal reasons, supporters are the reason he plays professional football. I'm not sure I could mirror the dedication of the fans we had when I played for Manchester United: the English football season rarely plays out under blue skies and bright sunshine, yet week after week they'd be there, in the terraces, enduring the foul weather to get behind us. It wasn't unconditional support – it took only a couple of goals conceded to learn some colourful Mancunian phrases – but whether they were cheering us on or helpfully pointing out where they felt we might be able to improve, the fans were there, in United colours, supporting us.

And it was the same with Everton, Spurs, Liverpool, Aston Villa, Newcastle and all of the other big clubs I came up against. It was also evident, albeit in reduced numbers, in the smaller clubs. I remember playing away to Colchester in the fifth round of the FA Cup in 1979 and experiencing for the first time the passion that exists in the lower leagues.

Across the world, football has an emotional hold on people like no other sport. As players, you can only respond positively to that emotional investment,

Across the world, football has an emotional hold on people like no other sport

and feel an obligation to return that investment on the field.

Support is a vital ingredient of success in both football and business. Support is not just something to be found in teamwork; it is something larger and more holistic that involves everyone who has an impact on the football club or on your business. In themselves, supporters are crucial to the success of a team, not only in the

Support is a vital ingredient of success in both football and business

boost they provide when backing their side, but also in the negative impact they can have when they turn against a manager or owner – think of Blackburn supporters calling for Steve Kean to go at the end of the 2011/12 season.

Or, in a peculiarly modern illustration of fan power, there's United midfielder Darron Gibson, one of the club's peripheral players, who shut down his Twitter account just hours after setting it up, such was the torrent of abuse he received from fans gleefully seizing the chance to hurl invective directly at him. (Many of those critics were United fans; support in football is indeed far from unconditional.)

The fans are illustrative of a broader aspect of leadership and success: the essential support roles played in all organisations by people other than the actual leader. In football that might be the first-team coach, the physios, the groundsman or the team bus-driver; in a business environment, it's your line managers and foreman, secretaries and personal assistants. Whatever the role, each person is a member of the team, part of the support structure. Sir Alex was very big on inclusivity – discussions were always about 'us' or 'we', rather than 'me' or 'you'. Closing the gap between members of a team is crucial to fostering a structure of support, no matter where a person sits in an organisation's hierarchy.

Whether putting together or maintaining an effective team, it is imperative to consider carefully the words you use. I challenge you to listen to the comments made by Sir Alex and his management team and to note where they talk about themselves and their achievements. You won't find such talk easily. It's simply not the accepted way at Old Trafford – there, it's all about the team.

This might seem a trivial point, but words carry huge weight and power within our psyches. Think of the words your parents or teachers may have used to criticise you, words like, 'You'll never amount to anything,' or, 'You make my life a misery.' Wounding phrases like these remain deeply lodged in our memories. That's one of the reasons why I end every conversation on the phone with my daughters by saying I love them always and forever (I take a slightly more masculine approach with my son) – I never want them to doubt that they are the greatest gifts in my life, and I know that these words provide a firm foundation of love and unconditional support in their lives.

> *This might seem a trivial point, but words carry huge weight and power within our psyches*

If words are powerful, why don't we use them more carefully and selectively in the workplace? Positive or negative comments about our work can also be remembered for life, but so can criticism delivered in a firm but positive way. Constructive criticism with pointers to areas for improvement can ultimately lead to praise on implementation of that advice; thus support in this form is essential, and this goes for every member of an organisation.

If words are powerful, why don't we use them more carefully and selectively in the workplace?

Of all the great names to have passed through Old Trafford, few are remembered more fondly by the players than Norman Davies. For most, his name probably won't ring a bell: Davies was the kit man throughout my time at United, a backroom general who somehow managed the entire club's playing kit and all the logistics involved. You've almost certainly seen him on television – he was the staff member who escorted Éric Cantona off the field in the infamous kung fu game against Crystal Palace. He was an indispensable part of the United team. Every club and business has its own Norman Davies.

What Davies represents, like the fans, is the support network without which no leader can hope to succeed. But as Darron Gibson's ill-fated flirtation with Twitter suggests, support is a two-way street and it can't be taken for granted. I remember with a grimace playing away in 1983 to Bournemouth, then managed by one Harry Redknapp in his first major coaching role. We'd arrived as FA Cup holders at a tiny ground that resembled our training facility, with change rooms that had a few hooks for clothes and little more. There's no doubt we'd turned up arrogantly expecting to trample our opponents; instead, we lost 2-0 to a team from the third division and were knocked out of the cup in the third round, with me missing a cross that led to one of the goals.

But if the loss was unexpected, then the media reaction was an even more unpleasant shock: one of the newspapers produced a pull-out with pictures of the team, each one of us (barring Bryan Robson) with an axe to the head. I was certainly among those to blame for that defeat; against Ipswich in 1980, the situation was different. It's rare that a goalkeeper faces three penalties in a single game, unless that game goes to a shoot-out. Not only did I face three that day, but I saved all three of them. Usually that would have been cause for enormous celebration; unfortunately, despite my heroics, we lost that match 6-0 – proof, then, that one person succeeding in a team is no guarantee of overall success, for if the whole team isn't working, individual triumphs might not be enough.

Just as playing attractive, winning football appeases the terraces, so your business has to deliver strong product to satisfy customers, good results to placate shareholders and a positive, supportive working environment to keep employees happy. Leadership encourages customers, shareholders and employees to buy in to the leader's vision, to understand objectives and to turn an individual vision into a shared one – a process closely linked to the issue of destiny, which was discussed in the previous chapter. It's this type of support, Professor Sondhi argues, that is of particular consequence:

> *Trust is developed through honesty and consistency in relationships*

Rarely is winning down to just one individual; even in sports like tennis or golf there are coaches, managers, psychologists and physiotherapists. Support is gained by building trust and having faith in the other people who make up the team, and trust is developed through honesty and consistency in relationships.

Sometimes the truth may make people unhappy, but if the feedback you're providing is honest and given in a gentle manner, you're creating an environment in which trust may flourish.

In teams, trust is further built by individuals admitting their weaknesses and mistakes, recognising the skills and experiences of other team members and being comfortable asking others for help. Gary spoke earlier in the book about Sir Alex doing exactly that with members of his staff and former players. He also mentioned asking for advice from a fellow speaker at a conference, and not getting the answer he might have wanted – but it turned out to have been the one he *needed*, and that's what support is all about. Trust involves giving team members the benefit of the doubt as well as ensuring that discussions are focused on appropriate issues. This, once again, is related to self-awareness and emotional intelligence, and not allowing personal feelings to cloud the issue.

In addition to the support that comes from people, other elements are also required to achieve sustainable success. This includes systems and processes that ensure continuity and advancement, and a structure that maximises the impact of the range of skills and people that comprise the teams. Think here of a football manager who has to use the best possible formation for his team, whether it's playing a lone striker up front, finding space behind the forwards for a creative midfielder, or utilising fast and dangerous wings.

What Professor Sondhi has just described is one of Sir Alex's greatest achievements at United: the implementation of the youth system and scouting network to create continuity and advancement. The long-term structures that United's manager has put in place have been a cornerstone of the club's success. Ajax Amsterdam remains the benchmark for youth development in Europe, and even though their players are being lured away to wealthier clubs at younger and younger ages, their second league title in a row in 2011/12 was a reminder of the value of youth development. Sir Alex was also quick to rid Manchester United of the drinking culture, something that had become an accepted facet of the club but that hindered the team's advancement.

I wasn't much of a drinker, but on a particular Sunday in 1985, with the club having won its first 10 games of the season, I was invited to lunch at an upmarket restaurant in Hale in Manchester. As England's regular second-choice keeper, I was part of the team's inner circle of senior players. And so I joined Bryan Robson, a legendary player and drinker; Norman Whiteside, the youngest footballer ever to play in a World Cup final (for Northern Ireland); Kevin Moran, an Irishman who could certainly hold his drink; and Paul McGrath, one of the finest defenders I've seen, who sadly became an alcoholic. Drinking sessions like the one on this particular Sunday surely didn't help him.

We met at 12.30 p.m. and the first round was ordered; Bryan and Norman promptly downed their pints in one gulp and ordered another each. Feeling a little peer pressure, I tried to do the same, and almost drowned. Determined to try to keep up, however, I nursed my way through six pints while the others cruised through 12 – and we still hadn't ordered any food!

With the Geordie, Irish and Belfast accents now slurred by 12 pints of lager, I was struggling to understand anything and excused myself for a three-hour 'rest'. I returned, though, as I'd promised, only to find the lads on number 18, barely managing to form words, never mind sentences. I choked down two last pints, and arrived at training the next day feeling atrocious ... but Bryan and Kevin were in top condition and tore into training as though they'd not had a single drink the night before.

They could somehow pull that off, and our manager at the time,

Ron Atkinson, had an approach that suited the hard-drinking senior core of players perfectly: you could drink as much as you wanted, as long as you were able to train properly the following morning. Ultimately that culture wasn't going to bring Atkinson the success he craved. Only when Sir Alex arrived and implemented an approach far more in keeping with the demands of the professional game did Manchester United's fortunes begin to turn around. Pockets of hard-drinking players created cliques within a broader group and gave the impression of being unprofessional, rather than a single, unified squad focused on shared success.

Every player at Old Trafford has to be a team player first, and then have all the extra ingredients to be chosen. If there's one sight that sums up this attitude, it's the substituting of players. I have rarely seen any player get substituted at Manchester United and show more than a hint of displeasure – the players understand that it's a squad game, with team members being rested for games or replaced whenever

Every player at Old Trafford has to be a team player first, and then have all the extra ingredients to be chosen

the manager feels necessary, and it's all done with a view to winning trophies. Contrast that with the behaviour of players from other teams when substituted – they throw their shirt to the ground, storm into the dressing room or even argue with the manager as they leave the field of play. The tolerance of that kind of selfish culture will rarely lead to sustainable success.

Creating a positive club culture is therefore essential. Patrice Evra has a very simple and effective way of describing United's ethos: 'Manchester United is a factory workers' club. You have to respect that culture. It's a club where we work hard.' José

Mourinho, for his part, creates team culture by insisting that all the players eat together and then remain at the table until the last person has finished. This he does to prevent cliques forming, as he believes that no player should place himself above the team or act like a star.

Similarly, Fabio Capello, the former England manager and a hugely successful club manager, wouldn't allow the England players to use PlayStations or mobile phones or to form cliques – everyone had to eat together, leave the table together and look smart both as individuals and as a group – in short, to do everything to generate the right kind of team spirit.

The obvious first step is to decide what sort of culture you want, and then to drive change from within the existing culture to the desired one. Investing in youth, developing a strong network of scouts, setting his sights very publicly on Liverpool's record number of league titles and clearing out the drinking culture that had become entrenched at the club – these were some of the elements of Sir Alex's approach. Not only was he clear in his vision, but he also made that vision clear to everyone else, and did so with enough passion and conviction to elicit the support he needed to carry him through some early hiccups. As Professor Sondhi makes apparent, this was critical for Sir Alex, as it is for all leaders:

The leader of a team needs to be clear about its direction. Without this clarity, focus suffers, as does support for the leader. The team needs to be viewed as a bus that is constantly moving forward, looking back only to learn lessons from past experiences. Not everyone will be in agreement all of the time, but the value of clarity and a (largely) unified vision outweighs the negatives of a minority in disagreement. (If the majority is in disagreement, however, then the vision might need to be reassessed – there's often a very fine line between an act of madness and an act of genius.) Some teams find it difficult to keep the longer term in view, perhaps due to short-term pressures, a lack of resources or a lack of realism in the goal. Again, having a clearly constructed picture of the perceived future allows for more committed buy-in and support from all involved.

The team needs to be viewed as a bus that is constantly moving forward, looking back only to learn lessons from past experiences

Succession planning and progression are also key to driving a team forward, as they ensure that team members don't get too comfortable with their success. The team needs to keep a constant eye on the longer term so that evolution is always on the agenda; this isn't something football has a history of doing well, but both Sir Alex and Arsène Wenger have strong records in this respect.

Less than a fortnight after they'd won the Champions League in 2012, Chelsea had already moved to strengthen their side, persuading Belgian midfielder Eden Hazard – at the time the hottest property in European football – that Stamford Bridge was a better choice than either of the Manchester clubs, which were supposedly his two other chief suitors. Aware that their conquest of Europe couldn't entirely disguise a sixth-place finish in the Premiership in the same season, Chelsea sought immediate improvement in the aftermath of their win over Bayern Munich. That type of action has become the norm in the professional game, and it is one that business should learn from. Football managers are constantly looking at new talent and planning beyond the season in question (always an optimistic move in football management ...).

Just as Chelsea snapped up Hazard, so Steve Jobs was already hard at work on the second version of the iPhone (the iPhone 3G) when the first incarnation hit the market. The speed at which the modern world operates has markets changing from minute to minute, and the competition is constantly on the lookout for opportunity or weakness. Leaders need teams who share the desire and hunger that Professor Sondhi places such value on below:

Successful teams possess players with a never-say-die attitude and an insatiable appetite for success. The leader needs to recruit people who mirror his or her own values. High-performance teams, while never enjoying failure, appreciate the lessons learnt from it and move on wiser for the experience. This attitude ensures that learning is constant.

The leader needs to recruit people who mirror his or her own values

Motivation of the individual is also critical in creating a shared team desire: there needs to be a fit between the individual's goals and the team's goals. This is particularly challenging in football, where only 11 players are needed to start a game, but more are required to cover for injury or loss of form, ensuring that the chosen 11 don't get complacent.

High-performance teams are characterised by progress and change, as they adapt and become more capable of attaining stated goals. They also need the flexibility to accept new members and integrate them as seamlessly as possible. Attrition in the workplace is unavoidable, and a company or business unit can't simply shut down because one member has departed. No matter who comes and goes, however, desire and hunger both ensure that the drive

High-performance teams are characterised by progress and change

in the team remains, and serve to alleviate some of the pressure on the leader, who then doesn't need to be the sole driving force at every moment.

That driving force does need to start somewhere, however. If you are the leader, you need to make sure that your enthusiasm, energy and sense of direction rub off on the rest of your team, just as Sir Bobby Robson did. Speaking of Robson after his death, José Mourinho recalled 'a man with an extraordinary passion for life and football, with extraordinary enthusiasm'. When Sir Alex set his Liverpool target, it wasn't just the fans who bought into the delightful prospect of overhauling their fierce rivals; the players also took up the cause, and the wave of self-belief that swept through Old Trafford kick-started the momentum that eventually enabled Sir Alex's goal to be reached.

How do you put yourself in Sir Alex's – or Sir Bobby's – shoes and turn yourself into a leader who has the capacity to inspire other people? It starts with inspiring yourself, and believing that your ambition, no matter how lofty, is within reach. If I'd been a nervous goalkeeper – or, rather, had I shown nerves – it would have negatively influenced my defenders and at the same time encouraged the opposition to think that I was a weak link. Perhaps that's why you see goalkeepers shouting at their defenders so often: it's a simple primal show of authority. The goal

If I wanted my teammates to believe in me, then I had to believe in myself and in my ability

was mine, and nobody was going to get past me – if I wanted my teammates to believe in me, then I had to believe in myself and in my ability. My focus on reaching every cross, stopping every shot and keeping out every penalty had to be complete, and, while I didn't always keep a clean sheet, that focus on excellence of performance afforded me the career I enjoyed at Old Trafford. It is this focus, according to Professor Sondhi, that allows leaders to communicate their vision and drive to the supporting team around them:

Provided that the goals are clearly defined and linked to the vision of the organisation, focus is essential to ensuring success. Flexibility is also required so that change happens at the appropriate time to deliver results. The leader ought to possess a range of characteristics, starting with a degree of emotional detachment – emotion needs to be removed from decision-making so that a more focused, balanced view is taken for the benefit of the team. Successful leaders tend to be accommodating of new and different ideas without losing focus: they are open to fresh input and creativity while keeping sight of the long-term goals and ensuring that they don't get compromised by short-term changes. It is imperative to stay grateful for what you have, but to welcome the challenge of improving on your status quo.

> *Emotion needs to be removed from decision-making so that a more focused, balanced view is taken for the benefit of the team*

The United teams I played for, while full of very talented individuals, combined as particularly effective sides. In part, that was down to the managers we played under, but I'd apportion considerable credit to the leaders within the team itself. Players like Mark Hughes,

Paul McGrath, Frank Stapleton, Bryan Robson and Norman White-side were hard, uncompromising footballers who didn't consider defeat to be an option. The 1985 FA Cup final is the ideal example of this: against an Everton team that had already won the league and the European Cup Winners' Cup that season, we went down to 10 men when Kevin Moran was sent off after 78 minutes. But we hung on with determination and a refusal to concede defeat. We took Everton to extra time, no goals conceded at either end, and 110 minutes into the game Mark Hughes took the ball wide before passing to Norman Whiteside, who, instead of heading for the corner to waste time and get us to penalties, where I felt we had a decent chance, decided to take on a defender instead.

I was screaming abuse at him for making what was clearly a crazy decision; the next minute, though, I was screaming with delight instead, as Norman had beaten the defender and scored a fantastic and deciding goal past one of the best keepers at the time, Neville Southall. Were we the better side that day? Certainly not with 10 men. But we were more determined, more committed, and had playing for us that day some of the best on-field leaders the English game has seen. That sort of leadership, Professor Sondhi concurs, is invaluable:

Leadership involves managing an environment of creative tension, whether it's goalkeeper and defender in robust conversation mid-game, or managers arguing over the merits of different marketing campaigns. Creative tension is needed to stretch the performance of team members, but strong leaders know which team members need to be stretched by applying pressure, and which members respond to a gentler approach. They will cater to the different personalities, all the while ensuring that the commitment and passion of the team as a whole is never compromised.

179

The objectives of leadership are to develop long-term sustainable success, to act in an appropriate manner and to encourage creativity. Successful leaders make decisions and believe in them; all actions are geared towards the single-minded implementation of those decisions. Success can mean many things. It's not necessarily the goal that makes you successful, but also the route that is taken in the attempt to achieve success. If you get your product to market as hoped, for example, but lose half of your staff in the

> *The objectives of leadership are to develop long-term sustainable success, to act in an appropriate manner and to encourage creativity*

process, has the goal really been achieved?

Interpretation of success can be broad: it can be judged on the innovation that's been employed to reach the goal; the degree to which an organisation's heritage has been respected; the selection of people involved in the support team and their contributions; the achievement of early-mover advantage; the strategy followed; and the demonstrated ability to change direction and adapt when necessary. One of the things that Sir Alex embraced when joining Manchester United was its history, its spirit – something he quickly realised was a valuable asset that couldn't be compromised. He has certainly succeeded in maintaining the heritage, spirit and strong support network of the club.

I mentioned Lucas Radebe at the start of this chapter. While he remembers the night he scored against Spartak with understandable joy, the smile vanishes when talk moves to the Leeds United of today. Champions League semi-finalists during Radebe's time at the club, Leeds had dropped to League One by 2007 (the old third division) after a spectacular financial implosion. At the end of the 2011/12 season, the club had managed 14th position in the Championship, an improvement on the division below, perhaps, but still some way off the heights of success achieved during Radebe's time at the club.

For all the top clubs, the financial stakes are now even higher and big investors expect the return that only Champions League success can deliver. Is this the way forward for the league in which I used to play? Traditionalists argue no; those with a modern view argue that big investment is the only route to survival. For me, a club with supporters at odds with its ownership is not in a tenable position in the long term: the fans who travel to away games and sit in the rain to watch their team grind out a result are doing so out of a love for what the club represents to them through its culture and history. An outsider arriving in a blaze of cash is not a naturally endearing figure, and bringing in star talent only goes so far in appeasing the faithful.

Will Manchester City's delighted supporters turn sour if the following years don't go so well? And will the wealthy new owners continue their support if success – which money can't guarantee in football – is not forthcoming? It places the English game, and the European game as a whole, in a fascinating position.

While the battle of the bank balances plays out, Professor Sondhi looks to America for alternative views on nurturing support for professional sport:

The Green Bay Packers in America's National Football League (NFL) offer an interesting counterpoint to the brash spending of European football. The Packers are no small community team, certainly – they've been extremely successful in a league where money is just as free-flowing as it is in European football – but they have worked hard to create not only a team spirit, but also a true community spirit. This has been achieved by ensuring that the owners of the team are all local members of the community, and no one owns more than 200 shares. Additionally, no dividends are paid – all profits are ploughed back into the club. It's a model that is anathema to the current trend in the Premiership, but one that has fostered a significant level of community support for the team. Still based in Green Bay in Wisconsin, the ownership model and the support it engenders are clearly working in the modern competitive arena: in January 2011 they won the Super Bowl, overcoming Pittsburgh in the final.

The Green Bay Packers example, though extraordinary, is an isolated one, and it's a romantic notion to imagine it playing out in the Premiership. But the principle is one worth remembering, and not just in the business of football. Industrial action has become common throughout Europe as workers protest the closing down of factories as they move to countries with cheaper labour and infrastructure costs. When the brand in question has a strong link to the country's heritage – and a number of British automotive brands spring instantly to mind – the parallel with new football ownership becomes strong indeed.

Building support is part of broader business decisions that take into account the nature and power of the support base. Does following a particular path, such as outsourcing operations or bringing in foreign labour, have a negative impact on your staff, your customers or your shareholders? Usually it's the staff who are of chief concern. Football clubs have vocal supporters who can quickly rally together, while workers have unions that play a similar role. Sometimes shaving money off the bottom line in the short term doesn't pay off in the long term – lose the support of your staff or your customers, and the damage may well be greater than the savings accrued. Thus, ensuring that you don't alienate your support base is another important element of leadership. To that, add the importance of keeping those supporters upbeat and committed when things aren't going well.

> *Ensuring that you don't alienate your support base is another important element of leadership*

I was fortunate to be at United during a time of reasonable success: two FA Cup victories, several strong finishes in the league and a 2-0 win over Liverpool in the charity shield in 1983. (That Liverpool side included Ian Rush, one of the most deadly strikers the English game has seen. I'm proud to say that in all of our clashes with Liverpool, Rush never scored against me – although plenty of his teammates did …) But the nature of the game means that you have lean runs, unexpected defeats, periods of a season that are as bleak as the weather outside. Those are the times that question the patience and resolve of the fans, show the spirit of the players and are a true test of the manager's mettle. The dressing room after a loss is a sombre place to be.

Looking back, I'm not sure I've ever felt as low as I did when we lost to Arsenal in the 1979 FA Cup final, having scored two late goals to draw level, only for me to miss a cross at the death, allowing Arsenal to score the winning goal. Dealing with that sort of blow at a personal level is immensely challenging; when you have to deal with your team as well, and keep your supporters' mood from sinking, you have a situation that, once again, as Professor Sondhi shows, calls forward Sir Alex by way of example:

Success shouldn't necessarily be seen as winning all the time. There's nothing wrong with winning all the time, but it's not a realistic ambition for either a football

Success shouldn't necessarily be seen as winning all the time

realistic ambition for either a football team (whatever certain Russian owners may believe) or a company. But the ability to persist with a cause despite defeat is a mark of success. One of the outstanding features of Sir Alex's leadership is the manner in which he responds to tough situations. Defeat to Barcelona in the 2010/11 Champions League final was an example of this: after acknowledging Barcelona's performance as being deserving of the trophy, Sir Alex proclaimed the Spanish side as Europe's best and made them the benchmark on which United needed to improve. Drawing inspiration from defeat, he was able to recalibrate his team's goals based on the performance of a rival, taking a positive result away from the loss. He did the same again after only just losing out to Manchester City in the league in 2011/12, and immediately setting the target of winning back the Premiership trophy from City the next season.

Sir Alex has used many a tough moment to inspire his players. Ryan Giggs talks about losing 2-0 at Liverpool to hand Leeds the title in 1992, and how the Anfield faithful were in raptures over having dealt this blow to their bitter Manchester rivals. Giggs said, 'After the game, as I was making my way to the team coach, a couple of Liverpool fans asked me for my autograph. I obliged, only for them to tear it up in front of me. The manager [Sir Alex] always reminds me of that incident to motivate me when we play Liverpool.' A leader needs to use all the available motivational tools, especially from setbacks, to inspire his or her team to achieve greater success.

Sir Alex isn't the only one to have managed such situations well. At Chelsea, Roberto Di Matteo took the turmoil of a sacked predecessor and used it to rally both players and supporters around him. While the league finish was modest by Chelsea's high standards, winning the FA Cup and the Champions League in 2012 was an outstanding response from manager and

> *A leader needs to use all the available motivational tools, especially from setbacks, to inspire his or her team to achieve greater success*

club. The nature of the performances in both the UEFA Champions League semi-finals, where Barcelona were heavy favourites, and the final, where Munich were tipped to win at home, speaks volumes of the resolve Di Matteo instilled in the Chelsea squad.

Arsène Wenger has also picked up his Arsenal side on numerous occasions. Similarly, a little further down the league, Roberto Martinez needed all of his guile and managerial skill to keep Wigan in the Premiership at the end of the 2011/12 season. And every season managers just stave off relegation, to the relief of nervous fans, or do get relegated and have to deal with the depression. It's a horrible place to be, but it's part of management. It's a situation that many people in business will identify with. Falling sales, rising costs, growing competition: in the tough economic climate we live in today, doing business isn't easy. But by taking seemingly negative situations and finding ways to turn them around, as well as to provide impetus to improve you, your team and your support structures, you'll be heading in the right direction.

You need to inspire your team, but you need to get some of that energy back from those you're working with. Professor Sondhi clarifies:

One of the key roles of the leader is to provide a stable environment for the individuals to be able to express themselves fully; this, effectively, is the return on investment for the leader from his or her team.

The way in which a leader demonstrates his or her values and vision behaviourally is a primary means of creating team spirit. Leaders in sport instil a passion in both the players and the supporters – picture any manager you like charging out from the bench to exhort his players to greater efforts, admonish those not giving their all or politely point out to the referee that he may have erred. Such naked passion spills over into the stands, catches the imagination of the fans and makes the world believe that nothing at all is more important to the manager than his team. Managers are thus catalysts in a team's support.

Leaders in sport instil a passion in both the players and the supporters

Historically, managers such as Bill Shankly at Liverpool, Bertie Mee at Arsenal, Sir Matt Busby at Manchester United and Bill Nicholson at Tottenham in the 1960s and 1970s were responsible for creating this community spirit at their clubs, often in difficult times. Is this the case today? How many of the growing dynasties actually aim for the long-term sustainability that Sir Alex has created? Nowadays the growth of long-term success is more the responsibility of the owners than the manager – gone are the days of a Sir Matt Busby building an enduring empire.

Teams generally fail to achieve their objectives for one or more of the following reasons: a lack of conviction in their own ability; barriers to team members' personalities being expressed within the team; weak organisational values are in place; or an attitude to risk that doesn't bring out the best. Dealing with these failings begins with building team spirit – constantly reinforcing positive mental states, encouraging team players and convincing them that they do add value. Team players behave in different ways, and leaders have to be sensitive to the different personalities. This can be achieved only by spending time with team members, something that sports leaders do through the process of coaching, where they begin to understand the development areas of the individuals.

> *Team players behave in different ways, and leaders have to be sensitive to the different personalities*

Personalities need to be encouraged within teams rather than shut out. Many organisations and sports teams find it uncomfortable to have a 'character' in their team and leaders generally try to limit their maverick elements, thus inhibiting their uniqueness. Top leaders, who are very comfortable with themselves, will encourage these characters and in many cases build their teams around these individuals. In this regard, Sir Alex's management of Éric Cantona has already been discussed at length. But, as Roberto Mancini discovered with Carlos Tévez and Mario Balotelli in the 2011/12 season, sometimes a firm hand is needed to keep people in check. Having said that, Tévez refused to play for him again after being disciplined, Mancini relented and the Argentinean striker played a key role in City's league triumph. Whether that short-term decision will pay off in the long-term relationship between Tévez and the club remains to be seen.

Finally, great teams and leaders are remembered for the chances they have taken, the risks that elevated them to hero status. Firm self-belief is essential to stretch the boundaries and grow the expectations of stakeholders, and leaders need to recognise their role in taking chances. The potential growth of a team or individual lies in the ability to take a risk, and then to believe in it. It won't always pay off, but unless you take the chance, you'll never know where it might have led you.

> *Great teams and leaders are remembered for the chances they have taken, the risks that elevated them to hero status*

I took a chance as young, naive goalkeeper heading over to England. I bought my own ticket, got onto an aeroplane (my kids are still convinced that in 1978 you had to sail to England) and set off to seek my fortune. But while the element of risk was undeniable, I also had considerable support: from my family, my friends and my coaches. The lessons I've learnt on the subject of support insist that, above all, it has to work both ways. I needed to perform to make sure I deserved the support of United fans. Sir Alex has had to deliver at Old Trafford to build up the devoted following he can now call upon.

New club owners have to understand that buying a football team is far more than just another business transaction. And leaders and businesses need to realise that the first step towards inspiring loyal and committed employees, workers, team members –

> *You can't cry over a lack of support if you've done nothing to earn it in the first place*

call them what you will – comes from the person at the top. You can't cry over a lack of support if you've done nothing to earn it in the first place; if you can't inspire other people to believe in your dream and share in your vision, then you have to ask whether you have enough belief in yourself. Footballers face that challenge every single day; embrace it yourself, and see where your employees take you.

TRAINING DAY

Support refers to both the human and the organisational resources that are available to a leader. No single individual is able to reach the final pinnacle of success in today's world due to the increasing complexity of the working (or sporting) environment, which means that standards and expectations are constantly being raised. To achieve success under pressure, leaders need to ensure that the best people, with the right skills and competencies, are in place, and that they create as much positive support around themselves as possible.

FULL-TIME TAKEAWAY

1. Build maximum support around you – start by using words such as 'we' and 'us' (not 'I' and 'me'), which will help to create a feeling of teamwork at a deep and meaningful level.
2. Build a support structure for sustainable growth and advancement (for example, youth structure in football, ending a drinking clique, etc.).
3. Ensure that you build the winning culture that works for you – hard work, appetite for success and ability to turn defeat into inspiration.
4. Build trust by being honest and consistent, but in a fair and gentle manner – when trust is able to flourish, then team members are more likely to ask and give help to each other.
5. Drive your progress forward with change – in the form of new team members and the use of the latest ideas, for instance.
6. Finally, sell your vision to your support structure by being clear and passionate about your envisioned future.

7

Conclusions and Change

'That is why to have been at
the top for more than 30 years is
proof of how strong Alex Ferguson is.
Life at the top can make people very
tired. The old man who wants to win
every game can only be admired.
He deserves a statue at Old Trafford.'
– *José Mourinho*

No matter how many times you've played for your team, the build-up to a game doesn't change. The night before, the nervous energy starts to kick in. Everyone has their own way of dealing with it: watch some television, play cards, read a book (the latter a rarely chosen option, granted). In the old days, the occasional player might have snuck in a drink to take the edge off. I remember my old roommate Garry Birtles telling me that when he was at Nottingham Forest, his manager, Brian Clough – one of football's great characters – insisted on buying Garry two pints the night before each game to ease his nerves. I'm not sure that would happen today.

Before you know it, it's match day, and the nerves of the previous night have intensified. You're starting to envision the game ahead, the opposition and the possible outcomes of the match. You're still doing that when it's time to leave for the ground; the team bus is an odd mix of nervous laughter, bravado and focus. Players are listening to their Walkmans (remember them?) or staring out towards a vague horizon, contemplating the challenge in store.

And suddenly you're inching through crowds to get to the ground, fans dressed in red and cheering you on, or wearing rival colours and hurling abuse at you with as much energy as they can muster. Finally, as pre-match tension hits its peak, you are in the dressing room, part of the starting XI, just moments away from 90 minutes that will end in either delight or despair. It's a wonderful, terrifying time, the tunnel and the dull roar of the crowd ready to welcome you to the awaiting battle.

That's exactly where you find yourselves now: in the dressing room, kitted up, ready to take the field. It's Wembley, and you're through to the Champions League final; awaiting you at the home of English football, your opponents tonight are Barcelona. Lionel Messi's coming in off the back of a hat-trick in the semi-final to knock out Manchester City. Andrés Iniesta's been imperious all season. Cesc Fàbregas is being tipped as La Liga's player of the year. And who do you have in your corner to cheer you on, guide you through the final and hopefully watch you emerge as manager of Champions League winners? Gary Bailey ...

Given the footballing context of this book, it seems appropriate to treat this final chapter as the pre-match dressing room. Together with my first-team coach, Professor Sondhi, I have spent the preceding chapters preparing you, training you and equipping you with the skills necessary to succeed under pressure and create the destiny you have within you. That destiny now lies 90 minutes away, so how do we sum up what we've said and give you that one final shove in the right direction? In short, how do we give you the perfect team talk that will send you sprinting down the tunnel and out onto the magical turf of Wembley to tear Barcelona apart?

I'd start with one simple, all-encompassing word: *change.* Adaptability and its importance have been discussed at length, and for good reason, but with the word 'change', I am looking beyond that. I'm referring not simply to the need to adapt to new situations or react quickly and efficiently to an environment that's constantly shifting, but to the understanding that if you want to reach your destiny,

If you want to reach your destiny, you have to make a conscious decision to reinvent your attitude and approach to life

you have to make a conscious decision to reinvent your attitude and approach to life. In short, I am talking about the need to welcome change, for if you do so you will successfully convert your dreams into your destiny.

Change your style of leadership to embrace the 'level-five leadership' discussed in Chapter 2. Change the nature of your interactions with people to develop and maximise your emotional intelligence. Move away from rigid thought patterns and inflexible structures to become the leader who can adapt seamlessly to an unpredictable environment. And do all of that as you seize hold of your own destiny and become your own navigator, rather than trusting fate to get you where you idly dream of one day going, and so decide how you want to be remembered.

As one of the greatest managers of all time, Liverpool's Bill Shankly replied when asked how he wanted to be remembered: 'Above all, I would like to be remembered as a man who was self-less, who strove and worried so that others could share the glory, and who built up a family of people who could hold their heads up high and say – WE'RE LIVERPOOL!' What a humble and yet inspiring vision!

In order to help you understand the process discussed in this book, I have tried to think back to what I did to face the change of leaving university in sunny South Africa and attempting to become a professional footballer in rainy Manchester. Nineteen years old and with a head full of wild teenage excitement, it was the period of my life that defined my destiny. Although I didn't realise that at the time, I did know, even then, that it was a move I had to make if professional football was going to be a serious objective of mine.

The first step in making the move was to be excited about the change and to welcome it, to see playing professional football in Europe as a unique opportunity to test my abilities and to challenge myself as an individual. Yes, there was the pressure of trying to make the cut, but rather than feeling overawed by that pressure, I was drawn to the desire to prove myself. Once I had signed for Manchester United, the initial excitement died down – not difficult when sharing a bedroom with two other aspirant footballers and no heating in the middle of winter, and then catching two buses to training every morning.

It was a case of being tough and keeping my energy levels and motivation high – which I did by being grateful for the opportunity to play (even if it was in the fourth team) for such a great club, and to experience living in a different country and climate. Gratitude, which has been discussed at length in this book, allowed me to relish the opportunities that I'd been given.

My next step was to observe carefully what I had to learn to reach my aim of being the number-one goalkeeper – learning to deal with wet, slippery balls, and judging the flight of crosses at sea level, and coated in mud (as opposed to crosses in Johannesburg, which is 6 000 feet above sea level, so

Gratitude allowed me to relish the opportunities that I'd been given

the ball – which is generally dry and rock-hard – flies a lot quicker).

Then I had to remain active and stay fitter than anyone else. We had a canteen at the training ground that served greasy fish and chips every day, so I would often go home to make something healthier, and I swam at a nearby pool to keep up my general fitness. I also had to manage my emotions, and that was an area in which I battled – I lost a huge amount of energy trying to bridge the culture gap from full-time university student to professional footballer. All of my colleagues played snooker and darts most of the day, and they drank a lot. That just wasn't me. I didn't want to adjust, as I felt it wouldn't further my aims, so I continued to study part time and completed a physics degree in Manchester while playing professionally. This was frowned upon at the club, as I was seen as trying to be better than everyone else and not fitting in with the team spirit.

That, in fact, wasn't the case – I've always strived to be a team player and recognise the importance of the unified collective – but the perception among my teammates remained otherwise. The inability to handle the emotional side of my differences with the majority of the team eventually resulted in my not enjoying my football, despite having played for three years. After nearly

100 games behind me, I started to play some really poor matches, which led to a loss of confidence. At one stage I thought of leaving United to continue my career on the continent (preferably in the sun by the sea) so that I would find more joy in my game. In the end, I didn't move. For all the challenges I was facing, I realised that the only person who could address and overcome them was me, and that playing for Manchester United was the destiny I'd dreamt of. I didn't want to give up on it.

> *For all the challenges I was facing, I realised that the only person who could address and overcome them was me*

As much as you might not enjoy them at the time, those darker periods offer invaluable lessons if you're willing to learn from them. Yes, it was cold, the club culture clashed with my own and I felt a certain sense of isolation. But I was the starting goalkeeper with the biggest club on the planet, and I had an enormous amount to be grateful for. Armed with that sense of gratitude and an awareness of the opportunity I was being afforded, I overcame the negative sentiment, focused on the enjoyment I derived from playing for Manchester United and became a better player for it. The learning part of change is crucial: once you have realised what it is you need to improve on, you need to undergo the learning process. The example of my learning provided earlier – when I needed to toughen up after being given a lesson in street fighting by Gordon McQueen – is a perfect example of changing to be more effective within your situation.

> *As much as you might not enjoy them at the time, those darker periods offer invaluable lessons if you're willing to learn from them*

Finally, you need support during a process of change, as we've shown in detail in this book. Again, this was one area that I couldn't get right in Manchester, and it also led me to think that I might need to leave for a sunnier country, one where they had a winter break (as the rest of European clubs do). I had left my family and friends behind and only got to see them once a year in the short summer break – a break made even shorter if I was on England duty, which I was almost every year. And during the summer break it was winter in South Africa, so instead of returning to a warm African sun, it was to the surprisingly bitter cold of Johannesburg.

Spending so much time away from home as a young man with no family and only a few new friends meant that I didn't have the support I needed while surviving in Manchester. That had a direct impact on my performance levels, which at one stage were not good enough and nearly resulted in my leaving the club. The goalkeeper is generally separate from the team, so I was often excluded from social gatherings or five-a-side games (I am, by my own frank admission, a woeful outfield player), and as a result I often felt ostracised.

How did I survive? I met a wonderful woman who was fun and inspirational, and who got me to enjoy the challenges I was facing and find a way to look forward to them. She created a feeling of family, friendship and fun, all aspects of my social life that had been sorely missed. This had an inevitable knock-on effect on my professional life.

I'd also spend many Fridays at the home for terminally ill children supported by the club; we all had to make a couple of visits a season, but I went as often as I could. Meeting children who were faced with death but who somehow kept smiling placed my own life in sharp perspective and cast off any self-pity I might have accumulated that week. It reminded me of just how good I had it, and why taking that for granted rather than being actively grateful for what I had was an extreme indulgence on my part. Needing to be grateful for playing at Manchester United might sound crazy, but we are all subjected to challenges, no matter how wonderful our work is or how good things are – we are human, and the principles of LEADS are fundamental to our continuing success – but what specific action steps can I give you in the heat of the moment that will help you implement LEADS?

Those steps can best be summarised by the acronym GREAT.

G – Gratitude, for all the wonders in your life. It helps you to make tough decisions.

R – Reframing your challenges to make them exciting.

E – Empathy, which begins with being observant.

A – Adaptability, which involves learning what you require to know in order to stay ahead and make the necessary changes.

T – Targets, which must be inspirational yet achievable.

As I'm speaking and the noise of the crowds outside the dressing room grows, I'll hand you over to the first-team coach to give his learned take on what I've just told you. And listen carefully: We have Barcelona to beat, and they won't make it easy …

After giving his presentations, Gary is always asked a variation of the same question: 'How do I incorporate these changes into my performance?' In designing the process of change, we've intro-duced a series of actions – described in each of the chapters – that helps in developing the high performer. Having coached and trained business people and athletes, however, we felt that it was important to talk about the process of change in a manner that's easy to understand – 'Simple enough for defenders, please, Rakesh' was Gary's directive to me. There are certain rules and facts that need to be observed and understood so that the benefits of the development programme are optimised.

There's a great quote from Muhammad Ali that sums up so much of what is required to effect meaningful change and explains why doing so is the exception rather than the norm: 'Champions aren't made in gyms. Champions are made from something they have deep inside them – a desire, a dream, a vision. They have to have the skill, and the will. But the will must be stronger than the skill.'

The point is that if you want to succeed under pressure, you need to *want* it! How many teenage prodigies catch the world's attention before falling back into anonymity? And how many teams have their star strikers and roving playmakers backed up by that hardworking holding midfielder who might not have the touch of Messi or Ronaldo but never stops running, tackling and hassling the opposition? Not everyone will be Messi or Ronaldo, just as not everyone will be Steve Jobs or Sir Richard Branson, but that doesn't mean they can't get to the top. A strong work ethic is probably the most valuable asset I've come across in both the corporate and sporting worlds.

> *The point is that if you want to succeed under pressure, you need to* want *it!*

Based on that simple philosophy, a few rules emerge that govern the process of implementing GREAT along with the process of change, starting from where we are now and ending when we've completed the necessary metamorphosis. That starts with one non-negotiable factor, without which the process is dead in the water: the individual has to *want* to change and must embrace the process. Have I mentioned welcoming the change? Yes, many times, and I'll do so again, many times more. The most consistent message I get back from audiences is how that simple mantra has fundamentally altered their approach to managing a business; more people who, like me, have discovered just how valuable a philosophy it is. As Davide Cardarelli, managing director of Nike South Africa, says, 'He who hides from risk, hides from its rewards.'

'He who hides from risk, hides from its rewards'

Gary's account of his own change when leaving the sun of South Africa to be welcomed by the rain of Manchester is a classic example of the importance of adaptability. Gary's root trait, however, was that he had the drive to be successful. He wanted to fulfil a dream, and that is the first principle of any change programme – desire. *The individual has to want to change.*

In the corporate world, there are many instances where leaders try to force change on their people, setting unrealistic deadlines and giving little consideration to the specific needs of the workforce. The reality is that if you want to see an individual change, they need to want it and to be able to understand the benefit of the process and the change it involves. If they fail to do so, there is simply compliance to a directive rather than actual commitment to the change programme. As mentioned in Chapter 2, the brain is capable of change and adaptation – science has long established this to be the case – but this can only be done if the motivation exists.

The next question is this: Can we develop this motivation to change? The answer is a simple, resounding, 'Yes!' Each individual has to be coached on the benefits of the change and, more importantly, how it positively affects them. Human nature leans towards the familiar, which is why 'comfort zone' is such an established term. It's understandable that we tend to opt for the safety of what we know rather than brave the unknown. But a comfort zone is the enemy of progress, growth and destiny. Individuals need to understand *why* they need to change and what the rewards of such change will be.

Once the concept of change has been embraced, it's crucial to understand the driving forces behind that change. We tend to find that there are many things we can change, but what we really need to understand is what the root cause of our behaviour is. Why do we think the things we do, and why is our perspective what it is? Why do we see the cup as being half full or half empty? Our response to a certain situation is dictated by our perspective.

From a sporting viewpoint, athletes are more comfortable with change and adaptation, as everything happens in a very short and specific time frame; reacting quickly becomes part of the job. In most cases, our perspective is shaped by our history and background, particularly our childhood – certain situations provoke a particular set of responses. Changing those responses isn't always easy: players will always protest to the referee when a penalty is given, but the decision is never changed. That situation has become part of the theatre of football, but it does also illustrate a uniform response ingrained in the behaviour of those involved. Exorcising that behaviour when it has been a part of us for so long is often the major obstacle in effecting change.

Extend that example to a team setting, and we still need to understand what the key drivers of the situation are. On joining Manchester United, Sir Alex saw that one of the issues was the drinking culture in the club. He identified the key culprits and moved them on; this acted as a trigger for the change process. Experience is a valuable asset, but in both football teams and businesses the older employee resistant to new methods, influences or management may prove detrimental to the team or company.

Pushing an established player or employee into a new space or new way of thinking equates to a movement outside of the comfort zone. Any form of development presupposes that you will step outside that zone – otherwise there is no development. A good coach knows how to take an individual outside of his or her comfort zone and bring them back to a place where they feel comfortable, but empowered by new skills, knowledge and responsibility.

In the early days of his time at Manchester United, as has been mentioned, Sir Alex made the team play in different structures and positions to develop flexibility and adaptability. Initially, many players found this challenging, but it had its rewards, as players became comfortable with changing roles as the need demanded. Today, Sir Alex employs the same practice, which is probably one of the reasons for Manchester United's having a stronger squad than first appears on paper. The Dutch concept of 'total football' was also discussed earlier in this book: while you wouldn't expect your accountant to perform the same role as your legal advisor or warehouse foreman, a degree of flexibility within an organisation is not just valuable, but increasingly non-negotiable.

> *A good coach knows how to take an individual outside of his or her comfort zone and bring them back to a place where they feel comfortable, but empowered by new skills, knowledge and responsibility*

To encourage that sort of flexibility, and to create a culture in which the shared vision is both fully understood and fully accessible, you need a precise formulation of that vision. If your goals or actions are too broad, then the brain's attention is diverted. By establishing set markers of behaviour, a leader in effect maps out what is required of a certain role. Arrive at a particular time, sign off on specified jobs, deliver reports to schedule: at both a personal and organisational level, rituals such as these provide the framework in which to operate. As they tend to occur at specific times, the brain quickly becomes familiar with a new routine and turns it into a habit.

When Sir Alex joined United, he understood the importance of creating new habits, particularly those habits associated with winners and champions. He was looking at creating a mentality informed by quality and attention to detail. An early example of this was getting players to wear smart suits before games, enhancing unity and pride in both the players themselves and in the team. It was a simple gesture, but a mightily effective one that is now used by sports teams all over the world.

It's important not to dilute the focus on a goal by throwing out too much during a period of change. Likewise, if the change is personal, don't try to take on everything at once: understand that change is a process, not an overnight transformation, and that giving different elements of that process time to settle is vital for overall success; in fact, it's well documented that about 30 days of practice will turn most actions, including GREAT, into a habit. Owing to the physical and mental effort required in adhering to rituals and achieving a specific task, the brain will struggle with more than one thing to focus on. Once a ritual has become a habit, the individual is ready to move on to the next challenge.

Change is a process, not an overnight transformation

A useful way of building focus is to write down what you would like to concentrate on most in strategic locations in your environment. This will act as a reminder of what takes priority. Additionally, what you've decided to focus on needs to be defined very specifically. As a completely random example, compare the statement, 'Read more books' to 'Read *Succeed under Pressure* by the end of this month.' The more general statement is open-ended and is likely to result in a loss of direction; the more specific one brings your objective into focus.

To be able to make the changes you've identified requires a period of reflection to see what works and why this is the case. Remember, change itself isn't cast in stone either – you might have decided on a new goal or direction, but frequently the change of tack opens you up to ideas or approaches that hadn't previously been considered. And so change itself is an agent of change. Think about that for a moment, and you'll probably be able to recall several occasions in your own life when exactly that has happened.

Change itself is an agent of change

Persisting with a new activity for a period of time can be quite demanding, both mentally and physically, especially in the early period of the change and development process. Greater gains are possible by taking a short break to allow recovery to take place. This period of recovery is very effective in allowing the changes to move to our subconscious, which makes the process simpler and faster the next time it's implemented. Research has shown that instilling a new habit in the brain takes approximately 30 days of continual practice, which points to the same message: allow yourself time to let change take effect.

Change demands self-discipline

Finally – and I can hear the referee outside, waiting for us to take to the field – understand that change demands self-discipline. If you've committed to it in the first place, then you have to see it through. Without self-discipline, you're defeating the purpose of what you have set out to achieve. The changes that this book has tried to encourage you to make are probably major and won't happen on their own. They demand energy, effort and focus to ensure that new traits become habits. Get someone to measure you and to hold you to your stated aims. For example, finding something new to be grateful for every morning for 30 days will create a powerful gratitude habit, but will take focus and energy in the course of a busy life to implement. The energy, effort and focus will pay off for you, just as they did for a 19-year-old kid who swapped the African sunshine for Manchester's drizzle and ensured that the greatest change of his life paid off spectacularly.

With kick-off minutes away and the opportunity for definitive success within reach, you have the summary of what's been explored in this book and the basic guidelines needed to plunge into the unknown. Except that now it's not quite so unknown: you should have a more than reasonable understanding of what obstacles to expect and how to go about overcoming them. By its nature, this book can't be a scientific instruction manual on the management and application of change, as every individual, team or company has different parameters and different destinies. It is the teams that I've followed as a broadcaster and commentator that offer more immediate examples of effective change.

Plenty has been said about the work Sir Alex has done at Old Trafford, but other clubs have experienced the process of change in recent years too. Liverpool have had to deal with American owners with a philosophy of sports ownership at odds with Anfield's history. Abramovich's takeover of Chelsea demanded a new level of performance from a club suddenly propelled to the front of the queue of football's wealthy aristocrats. Leeds United were forced to come to terms with a rapid fall from grace. And Manchester City have found their fairy-tale prince in the form of wealthy Abu Dhabi investors. In all of these cases, the process of change has been fast-tracked, and that may well influence the success (or failure) of that change over the longer term.

But for now, the more important considerations are the lessons to be learnt from the people discussed in this book, starting with Sir Alex but including a range of others, footballing and otherwise, whose examples offer insight into the art of succeeding under pressure. The LEADS structure helps outline the principles to cope with pressure, but the actual steps you need to take can be best summarised by the acronym GREAT – it's simple and useful to use, and not too difficult to remember.

This one word, 'GREAT', will help you to reach the heights that you have dreamt of, those that are your destiny. What's more, it will help you to handle and succeed under intense pressure. GREAT is based on simple philosophies and easy-to-implement strategies, but the key is to do them consistently and properly. Sir Alex has always done that – he is consistent in the standards he has demanded of himself and everyone around him. He is always

> *Sir Alex is consistent in the standards he has demanded of himself and everyone around him*

changing, trying new formations, looking to bring in new players and insisting on a hardworking, team-based culture at Old Trafford. He has achieved incredible success, but once his goals are reached he immediately moves on to the next challenge. He's dealt with loss and defeat by using it to inspire himself and his team to bounce back even stronger. Above all, he has worked very hard to achieve his goals. Dennis Irwin, a member vital to Manchester United's successes in the 1990s, reckons that Sir Alex's commitment and effort are the outstanding features of his character, and that because of this he has consistently performed – and succeeded – under extreme pressure.

And we're under pressure now, because it's almost time to send you out into a packed Wembley to square off against the might of Barcelona. So for one last time, here's Professor Sondhi, your splendidly able first-team coach, to offer final inspiration:

We've discussed some exceptional managers in this book, leaders who have each redefined the modern game in their own way. Sir Alex Ferguson, Sir Bobby Robson, Arsène Wenger, José Mourinho, Pep Guardiola ... But it's not their ability to pick up three points on the road that amazes me, or the perfect timing of exactly the right substitution; rather, it's their leadership qualities that catch my eye. These are qualities that I've seen in people like Steve Jobs, Sir Richard Branson and Indra Nooyi, business leaders who have made the world sit up and take notice of the way they've led by example, inspired those around them and transformed their working environments.

Jobs, Branson, Nooyi: the driving forces, respectively, behind Apple, Virgin and Pepsi. They are three leaders who might not be able to implement a 4-3-3 formation, or drop a key player into midfield to stifle the opposition's possession (although I have no doubt Branson would try). But, as Professor Sondhi has so astutely suggested, each one shares intrinsic leadership characteristics with the best managers I've played under or studied as a television pundit. They have a clear vision, they understand what they need to do to get there and they have the ability to bring the best out of the people they work with – and all the while they are under enormous pressure and constant scrutiny. And this analogy really does emphasise the central philosophy of this book: if the world's great business leaders share so many traits with football managers, then the men in the dugouts surely have much to teach us on the art of leading, and succeeding, under pressure.

If the world's great business leaders share so many traits with football managers, then the men in the dugouts surely have much to teach us on the art of leading, and succeeding, under pressure

But for all the lessons they can dish out, every manager will tell you the same thing: there's only so much other people can do for you. All the training, all the coaching and all the support is only useful if you take advantage of it, and that's what you now need to do. You might be the head of a Fortune 500 company; you might run a bakery in your local neighbourhood. Either way, the only person who can turn the dreams you have for yourself or your business into reality is you.

The hurt of losing the FA Cup in 1979 to Arsenal still haunts me, even though I know I learnt and grew from the experience. But the unrestrained joy of running round Wembley in 1983 after beating Brighton in the FA Cup final replay, trophy in hand, is an equally vivid recollection, and together these two memories form the opposite ends of the spectrum of my football experiences. Through that spectrum I've learnt, grown and been able to achieve a career and a personal life I reflect on with great pleasure: my time at Manchester United, my work on television, the talks and presentations I now give and, most importantly, the wonderful interaction I have with my awesome family.

As this book shows, throughout my life I've had to adapt and change to become a better, more successful person. I've had to take knocks and reframe my challenges, and I had to work really hard to engineer the destiny that began as a schoolboy dream of playing football for Manchester United.

That was my dream; right now, it's your dream that's the important one, and it's waiting for you to make it happen. We all have our own Barcelona looming on the horizon – the target we need to reach if the dream is to become destiny. Your dressing-room speech is done; your manager and coach have said everything possible to inspire you. Run out of the tunnel, take in the audience waiting to see how you perform and then pull off that victory. Be grateful. Be tough. Stay humble. Reframe challenges. Observe carefully. Adapt and learn. Build support. Finally, embrace the chance to make the change that puts your destiny on track for you to be GREAT, and the best version of GREAT that you can be. Put your Barcelona to the sword, and show yourself and the world how to succeed under pressure.

Bibliography

Ballou, R., D. Bowers, R.E. Boyatzis, and D.A. Kolb. 'Fellowship in Lifelong Learning: An Executive Development Program for Advanced Professionals', *Journal of Management Education* 23 (4), 1999, pp. 338–354

Bar-On, Reuven. *Bar-On Emotional Quotient Inventory: User's Manual*. Toronto: Multi-Health Systems, 1997

Bar-On, Reuven, and James D.A. Parker (eds). *The Handbook of Emotional Intelligence: Theory, Development, Assessment, and Application at Home, School, and in the Workplace*. San Francisco, California: Jossey-Bass, 2000

Cannon, Walter Bradford. *Bodily Changes in Pain, Hunger, Fear, and Rage*. New York: Appleton-Century-Crofts, 1929

Collins, J. *Good to Great: Why Some Companies Make the Leap ... and Others Don't*. New York: HarperBusiness, 2001

Cubeiro, J.C., and L.G. Guerrero. *Liderazgo Guardiola*. Alienta, 2010

Emmons, R.A., and M.E. McCullough. 'Counting Blessings Versus Burdens: An experimental investigation of gratitude and subjective well-being in daily life', *Journal of Personality and Social Psychology* 84 (2), 2003, pp. 377–389

Ferguson, A. *Managing My Life: The Autobiography*. London: Coronet, 2000

Giggs, R., and I. Ponting. *Ryan Giggs: My Life, My Story*. London: Headline, 2010

Gilbert, Daniel. 'The Science Behind the Smile', *Harvard Business Review*, January/February 2012, p. 88

Goleman, D. *Emotional Intelligence: Why It Can Matter More Than IQ*. New York: Bantam Dell Publishing Group, 1996

Holt, Oliver. *If You're Second You Are Nothing: Ferguson and Shankley*. London: Macmillan, 2006

Lencioni, P. *The Five Dysfunctions of a Team: A Leadership Fable*. San Francisco, California: Jossey-Bass, 2002

Lyubomirsky, S., L. King, and E. Diener. 'The benefits of frequent positive affect: Does happiness lead to success?', *Psychological Bulletin* 131, 2005, pp. 803–855

McClair, B., and J. Woolridge. *The Odd Man Out: A Player's Diary*. London: André Deutsch, 1998

Mourinho, J., and L. Lourenço. *José Mourinho: Made in Portugal – The Authorised Biography*. Stockport: Dewi Lewis Media Ltd, 2004

Neville, G. *Red: My Autobiography*. London: Bantam Press, 2011

Robson, B. *Robbo: My Autobiography*. London: Hodder & Stoughton, 2007

Robson, R. *Bobby Robson: My Autobiography – Farewell but not Goodbye*. London: Hodder & Stoughton, 2005

Sharpe, L. *My Idea of Fun: The Autobiography*. London: Orion Publishers, 2005

Sondhi, R.K. *Total Strategy*. BMC Global Services Publications, 2008

Whiteside, N. *Determined: The Autobiography*. London: Headline, 2008